The Art of Place

Date: 1/1/20

728.0973 LED
Ledbetter, Lee,
The art of place :
architecture and interiors /

PALM BEACH COUNTY
LIBRARY SYSTEM
3650 SUMMIT BLVD.
WEST PALM BEACH, FL 33406

The Art of Place

LEE LEDBETTER
ARCHITECTURE AND INTERIORS

EDITED BY MAYER RUS

FOREWORD BY JOHN STUBBS
INTRODUCTION BY MAYER RUS
PRINCIPAL PHOTOGRAPHY BY PIETER ESTERSOHN

New York · Paris · London · Milan

To my parents, Roy and Helen, who each in their own ways nurtured my keenness for nature and beauty.

And to Douglas, my husband, my prince.

CONTENTS

FOREWORD	11
INTRODUCTION	13
THE ARCHITECT'S HOUSES	
Dumaine Street	18
Marquette Place	32
HOUSES OUTSIDE THE CITY	
Bayou Bonfouca	50
Boxwood Court	66
Cherry Hill	84
Bayou DeSiard	102
APARTMENTS IN THE CITY	
Decatur Street	116
East End Avenue	124
HOUSES IN THE CITY	
Lake Pontchartrain	132
Esplanade Avenue	150
Chestnut Street	164
Sackett Street	178
Fisk-Hopkins House	194
CIVIC BUILDINGS	
Joan Mitchell Center	210
St. Charles Avenue Presbyterian Church	218
Sydney and Walda Besthoff Sculpture Garden	226
CREDITS	236
ACKNOWLEDGMENTS	239

PAGES 2–3 In the Sydney and Walda Besthoff Sculpture Garden, artworks by Robert Graham and Scott Burton are installed at a reflecting pool near a pedestrian bridge. **PAGE 4** A Bill Jacobson photograph and a Karl Springer table frame a sculptural staircase in the Lake Pontchartrain residence. **PAGES 6–7** Ceramic vessels are perched on cypress shelves fixed to a weeping mortar brick wall in the Marquette Place residence. **OPPOSITE** A vintage Paul Evans bar cabinet enlivens the study in the Sackett Street residence in Houston.

FOREWORD
BY JOHN STUBBS

LEE LEDBETTER AND I SHARE A HOMETOWN in Monroe, Louisiana, a small city nestled against the Ouachita River in the northeast corner of the state. The river and several bayou tributaries run through quiet residential areas that emerged from former cotton fields, where oaks and cypress trees beautifully frame the houses, many of which were designed by my late father, the architect William King Stubbs. My childhood home was less than a mile away from Lee's, although we did not know one another at the time. Fortuitously, our paths would cross years later in New York City, where Lee was working as a young architect and I was practicing and teaching architectural preservation, and part-time hosting salon-style gatherings at my Lexington Avenue antiquarian bookstore and gallery. Eventually, we would both land in New Orleans, again less than a mile apart.

It is exciting to see Lee's architectural designs being shared more widely in this handsome monograph. For me this portrayal of over three decades of his work illustrates a contemporary architecture that wisely extends the centuries-long classical tradition in Western architecture while remaining tethered to the vernacular traditions of the American South. Always mindful of functionality and clients' needs, Lee's work favors the quiet, elegant, and time-tested aspects of traditional architecture, even as it resonates with a wholly contemporary spirit. The results are anything but commonplace.

A sensitive and keen observer of art and architecture all his life, Lee has long understood the enduring principles of both classicism and modernism. All of his work is carefully considered, well-crafted quality architecture. Both his exterior and interior designs optimize space through his sure use of axial planning, scale, balance, and proportion. Lee is also a rare example of a modern architect who is seriously competent in "total design." An artist and collector in his own right, he has a fine eye for designing and assembling décor.

At the larger scale, Lee has a remarkable ability to fit his buildings into the context of his sites, whether it's a modern hilltop villa for a scion of the McIlhenny family at Avery Island or his flowing arrangement of artists' studios placed in the heart of a historic New Orleans residential block at the Joan Mitchell Center. His mastery in blending old and new in both architectural detailing and décor is eloquently expressed in his work at St. Charles Avenue Presbyterian Church in New Orleans. I especially admire Lee's wide-ranging rehabilitation projects, where he preserves the most distinctive extant designs and intervenes elsewhere in a respectful manner. His several New Orleans renovations prove this out, the best example being his own home, Marquette Place, a heroically preserved landmark in New Orleans modernism.

Ultimately, the buildings and interiors of Lee Ledbetter reflect his understanding and respect for the best of Western architectural history and the richness of the American South. At all scales his work both reassures and inspires.

An octagonal dining room is crowned with a 1960s Murano chandelier in the Cherry Hill residence on Avery Island in Louisiana.

INTRODUCTION
BY MAYER RUS

LEE LEDBETTER'S STORY IS ONE OF DUALITY. A serious architect who maintains an unapologetic passion for decorating, he is fluent in and respectful of both traditional and modern design idioms. His education and early professional experience straddled the orthodox, neo-Corbusian modernism of Richard Meier, Charles Gwathmey, and other members of the New York Five as well as the vernacular-inflected, non-doctrinaire architecture of Robert A. M. Stern, Michael Graves, and their fellow mandarins of postmodernism. Ledbetter is, at his core, a Southern gentleman, yet his worldview is unabashedly cosmopolitan.

Conventional wisdom among architecture purists posits an antithetical relationship between traditionalism and modernism. Devoted practitioners are expected not only to align themselves with one side or the other but also to develop a narrowly defined signature style that becomes their calling card. Ledbetter is having none of it. Far from diluting the power and quality of his projects, his refusal to pledge absolute allegiance to a single design approach is a source of strength. His work celebrates the heterogeneity of contemporary life by embracing the idiosyncrasies of site, context, and client. For Ledbetter, the integrity of any design is a function of its success in addressing a project's peculiar challenges. He insists that form-making divorced from the humanist imperatives of comfort and nurturing, no matter how artful or inspired, can never rise to the level of great architecture.

The myriad projects illustrated in this volume testify to the elasticity of Ledbetter's vision. Included are period-sensitive restorations of historic properties, ground-up houses that speak in contemporary dialects of traditional Southern design languages, startlingly modern structures, and gracious public works that pay homage to the past while celebrating the present. Still, the overall impression of Ledbetter's oeuvre is anything but schizophrenic. The through lines that unify his far-flung projects are clarity of conception, quality of construction, probity, and grace—not superficial style markers.

Of course, as the images in this book attest, Ledbetter's projects have style to spare. More than a half century after Frank Lloyd Wright issued his caustic indictment of "inferior desecrators," many architects continue to dismiss decorating as a second-class discipline lacking the intellectual rigor of their own heroic pursuit. Ledbetter has little patience for such outmoded chauvinism, which historically posited architecture as a masculine endeavor while demeaning the selection of furniture and fabrics as women's work. Ledbetter has always had an affinity for the decorative arts, and his willingness to self-identify as both an architect and a decorator—taboo for many practitioners—provides eloquent proof of the esteem in which he holds both disciplines.

The seeds of Ledbetter's unconventional aesthetic sensibility were planted during the architect's childhood in Monroe, Louisiana, a place redolent of Southern gentility and classic Americana. He grew up in a Georgian-style house replete with dormers, crown and dentil moldings, and dark green shutters. The interior of the home, however, had a decidedly more modern vibe, with recessed can lighting and stripped-down wood paneling. Courtyards and gardens nurtured his nascent fascination with plant life, flowers, trees, and all the

The entry gate and walkway at the Marquette Place residence, now owned by Lee Ledbetter and Douglas Meffert. The Nathaniel "Buster" Curtis–designed house is listed on the National Register of Historic Places.

other elements of landscape design. Beyond his own home, Monroe boasted a fine stock of traditional residences built from the 1920s to the 1940s, along with flat-roofed modernist houses. Ledbetter found them all equally inspiring.

Even as a child, the young aesthete demonstrated a marked sensitivity to his environment. He recalls annually redecorating his room with antiques and other furnishings purloined from different parts of his family home. When one of Ledbetter's brothers went off to college, and he finally commanded a bedroom of his own, his mother hired a decorator to renovate the space. In characteristically precocious fashion, he insisted on a chic black-and-white design scheme. When the decorator presented options for carpeting to his pubescent client, Ledbetter pooh-poohed the choices, instead presenting a photograph of Gloria Vanderbilt's bedroom from a 1970s issue of *Vogue*, which contained a carpet more to his liking. And so it went.

As an undergraduate at the University of Virginia, Ledbetter became enthralled with the study of architecture. Rather than approaching the subject as a dry exercise in mathematics and engineering, he began to look at architecture through the lens of art history, an idea supported by his teacher Bruce Abbey. That foundational perspective—architecture and art as inextricably linked and mutually ennobling forces—has informed Ledbetter's practice to this day. It's not by chance that painting and sculpture figure so prominently in his work, and that his résumé lists important projects for museums, arts organizations, and private collectors.

After leaving Virginia, Ledbetter spent a year in New York City at the Institute for Architecture and Urban Studies, where he studied under Diana Agrest, Aldo Rossi, Charles Gwathmey, Robert A. M. Stern, and other luminaries. Beyond the classroom, however, the city itself provided a separate education. This was Ledbetter's first experience living in a metropolis, and the lessons learned about the complexity, rigor, and precariousness of the urban fabric would prove invaluable when the architect established his own firm in New Orleans nearly a decade later.

Michael Graves, another architect deeply invested in the relationship of architecture to painting, guided Ledbetter's graduate studies at Princeton University. At the time, the hegemonic modernism that had dominated architectural discourse for decades had at last given way to other modes of expression, and Ledbetter immersed himself in the revolutionary *cri de coeur* of postmodern ideology. While the young architect thrived in the atmosphere of creative ferment at Princeton, he spent summers augmenting his academic experience with work at Graves's own practice, then at the height of its influence.

Graves's office proved to be a decidedly different environment than the one Ledbetter encountered at Skidmore, Owings & Merrill's Chicago office. He chose SOM and Chicago specifically to gain a more intimate knowledge of the architecture of Mies van der Rohe, whose work had been but a footnote in the curricula of Virginia and Princeton. To his surprise, SOM in the mid-1980s had moved away from the gospel according to Mies in favor of what Ledbetter describes as bland corporate historicism. He soon returned to the East Coast, and in the offices of Harry Wolf (who was then practicing with Thomas Phifer) and later Gwathmey Siegel, Ledbetter absorbed a reverence for purity of detail and honest expression of intersections between different materials—two hallmarks of high modernist design.

Eventually, Ledbetter's more wide-ranging tastes landed him in the office of Robert A. M. Stern, where he received an education nonpareil in American regionalism and vernacular styles. Ledbetter credits Stern with teaching him how to design rooms around the furniture they require as well as the lives of the clients that inhabit those rooms—essentially a more humanist approach to design that privileges suitability, function, and comfort over style.

Artworks by Andy Warhol and chairs by Pierre Paulin strike a pose in a new family room at the Boxwood Court residence in Monroe, Louisiana.

After five years with Stern, Ledbetter returned to Louisiana, as he always imagined he would, to establish his own practice. In 1995, he hung his shingle in his mother's hometown of New Orleans, a city rife with architectural character and opportunities to renovate, restore, and build. Early on, Ledbetter grappled with the question of how his training, particularly in neo-Corbusian modernism, might apply to work in a place as tradition-bound as Louisiana. He wondered if there was even an audience for modern architecture or if he'd feel pressured into conjuring slavish reproductions of historical models.

Relying on lessons learned from Graves and Stern, Ledbetter consciously rejected the antiquated distinctions between historicism and modernism, choosing instead to forge his own path. One of his earliest projects—a bayou house for artist George Dunbar—made a compelling case for the synthesis of the past and the present. A contemporary interpretation of the vernacular architecture indigenous to southern Louisiana, the house draws inspiration from the steep-roofed Creole dwellings that proliferated on farms and plantations before the Civil War. By utilizing architectural details abstracted from relevant archetypes, and by marshaling those details in response to the verdant site, Ledbetter conjured a vision of modernity unashamed to celebrate its inheritance from history. The success of the endeavor garnered national attention for Ledbetter's fledgling practice.

Another early residential project provided an object lesson in the importance of integrating architecture and interiors. Ledbetter spent two years working on the house before the clients brought in a decorator to furnish his rooms. The results were disjointed and less than thrilling. To maintain the integrity of his work, Ledbetter determined that interior design must remain under his purview. For many modern architects, decorating simply means installing a few of Mies van der Rohe's Barcelona chairs in a pristine white cube. For Ledbetter, the art of interior design is in the pursuit of beauty, comfort, and appropriate scale. He outfits his projects with a kaleidoscopic mix of pedigreed antiques, spruce mid-century classics, sentimental items from his clients' personal collections, and impeccably tailored bespoke furniture.

Even as the mania for mid-century modernism reached a fever pitch in the past two decades, Ledbetter typically sidestepped the most predictable exemplars of the movement, choosing instead to focus on its more idiosyncratic masters. His touchstones are T. H. Robsjohn-Gibbings, Edward Wormley, Milo Baughman, William Haines, and Harvey Probber—designers who themselves made a convincing case that modern furniture need not abandon historical references and basic pleasure in the drive to avant-gardism. Ledbetter deploys these designers' creations in vivid ensembles that come alive with color, pattern, and rich texture— qualities often banished from the lexicon of high modernism.

Another hallmark of Ledbetter's practice is his dedication to establishing meaningful connections between architecture and nature. Like decorating, he views landscape as an essential component of holistic design, one with infinite potential to enhance the experience of a home, a church, or a museum. Whether he is designing an urban courtyard, a suburban backyard, or a house situated in a bayou wilderness, Ledbetter approaches landscape as an extension of the built environment—particularly in the balmy climate of the American South. His projects are marked by gracious transitions from indoors to out and vice versa, as well as a harmonic interplay between natural and artificial illumination.

Ultimately, Ledbetter's work is about elevating the quotidian rituals of daily life. He eschews strained theatrics and overly dramatic gestures in favor of subtlety and nuance. In an image-driven culture, where novelty and extravagance so often masquerade as virtues, Ledbetter remains steadfast in his belief that true style can only emerge from substance. Anyone fortunate enough to live in or visit one of the projects presented in this monograph will surely appreciate his dedication to that concept.

Artesian ponds with native flora meander through the site of artist George Dunbar's Bayou Bonfouca residence in Slidell, Louisiana.

DUMAINE STREET
FRENCH QUARTER, NEW ORLEANS

Thorough yet discreet, the renovation of this Greek Revival side-hall townhouse in the French Quarter was driven by the need to accommodate a wide-ranging collection of contemporary photography. Although the original architecture was strategically modified—mainly to facilitate a more gracious flow of space from room to room—great effort was taken to replicate millwork in keeping with the original architectural details.

Materials, finishes, and even furnishings were orchestrated to create a restrained, luminous backdrop for the art collection, which includes signature works by Lynn Davis, Hiroshi Sugimoto, Nan Goldin, Cindy Sherman, Adam Fuss, and Bill Jacobson. The home's original pine floors were refinished with an ebony stain and multiple coats of high-gloss lacquer to maximize reflection of light. The color palette for both walls and fabrics is largely neutral, again in deference to the photography on view. The hushed palette has the additional advantage of conjuring a sense of refuge from the chaos of the city.

Within the home's classically proportioned rooms, unfussy ensembles of vintage furnishings and accessories from the 1930s, '40s, and '50s allow plenty of breathing room for the photography collection, which encompasses both small-scale works and large, black-and-white imagery and color. Chairs and tables by the likes of Gilbert Rohde, Edward Wormley, and William Haines plumb the softer side of twentieth-century modernism; their neoclassical underpinnings subtly echo the architecture's Greek Revival lines. The main exception to the quiet understatement that pervades the house is the vibrant banana leaf wallpaper that creeps onto the walls of the kitchen in a sympathetic embrace of the lush greenery that unfolds in the adjacent garden.

PREVIOUS PAGES Artworks by Jacqueline Humphries, Christopher Bucklow, John Baldessari, and James Casebere coexist with mid-century modern furniture in this Greek Revival townhouse. **OPPOSITE** A Taccia lamp by Achille Castiglioni rests on a Ledbetter-designed étagère in a corner of the living room.

Artworks by Hiroshi Sugimoto, Adam Fuss, and Lynn Davis surround a vintage dining table by T. H. Robsjohn-Gibbings. The burl walnut and brass cabinets are by Donald Deskey.

Pairs of vintage chairs by Baker and T. H. Robsjohn-Gibbings share matching Edward Wormley occasional tables.

In the master bedroom, artworks by Wolfgang Tillmans, Richard Misrach, and Sally Gall surround a custom bed and a vintage Stark carpet.

ABOVE The kitchen's French doors and banana leaf wallpaper blur the distinction between inside and outside. **OPPOSITE** The courtyard was relandscaped with tropical vegetation.

ABOVE A David Hilliard photographic triptych fills the sitting-room wall. **OPPOSITE** Thick acrylic bookshelves and custom white oak consoles frame the fireplace and photograph by Nan Goldin.

ABOVE Red fish-patterned curtains and Eames chairs take their color cue from a Richard Caldicott photograph. OPPOSITE A vintage Edward Wormley bed, biomorphic table lamps, and 1970s geometric-patterned carpet share space in a guest bedroom.

MARQUETTE PLACE
UPTOWN, NEW ORLEANS

Nathaniel "Buster" Curtis of the famed New Orleans architecture firm Curtis and Davis—authors of the New Orleans Superdome and the IBM Building (now United Steel Workers Building) in Pittsburgh—designed this residence for his wife and seven children in 1961. At the time of its construction, the groundbreaking home was featured in several national magazines, including *Life*. Lee Ledbetter purchased the modernist masterpiece directly from the family sixteen years after Curtis's death. Ledbetter worked with the Curtis family in support of the building's listing on the National Register of Historic Places, making it the first modern residence in New Orleans—and the first project by Curtis and Davis—to be so recognized.

The house is designed as an inspired *pas de deux* of interior and exterior spaces individually expressed as solid and glass volumes. The main social areas occupy two glass pavilions sandwiched between four courtyards. In this latest renovation, the kitchen was brought up to date, and an adjacent breakfast room was transformed into a library/study. Lighting throughout the house was also updated to illuminate art. In the back bedroom pavilion, six children's rooms were reconfigured into a pair of guest suites and a master suite. The former master bedroom was redesigned to become a gym and den. Cabinet and door hardware and closet systems were salvaged and reused. All of the changes were closely coordinated with the National Register's review process.

The house's four courtyards underwent extensive renovation: fountains were restored, custom garden lighting was installed, and most of the plant material was replaced with native species. In terms of décor, the scheme was influenced by the dazzling green oaks and the ever-shifting panorama of white clouds and blue sky visible through the clerestory windows. To impart a corresponding liveliness to the interiors, period furnishings and a few antiques were judiciously added to a selection of classic mid-century furnishings original to the house, creating a more diverse, worldly mix. Many of the pieces were reupholstered in blue and citron-yellow fabrics that complement the red-orange hue of the existing walnut millwork.

PREVIOUS PAGES Ledbetter designed the cast glass and bronze cocktail table in the living room. The brick walls extend into an adjacent courtyard. **OPPOSITE** At the end of the largest patio, a glass hallway connects pavilions detailed with steel arches.

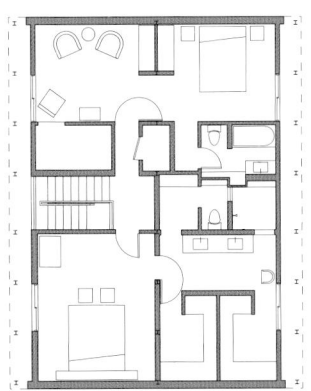
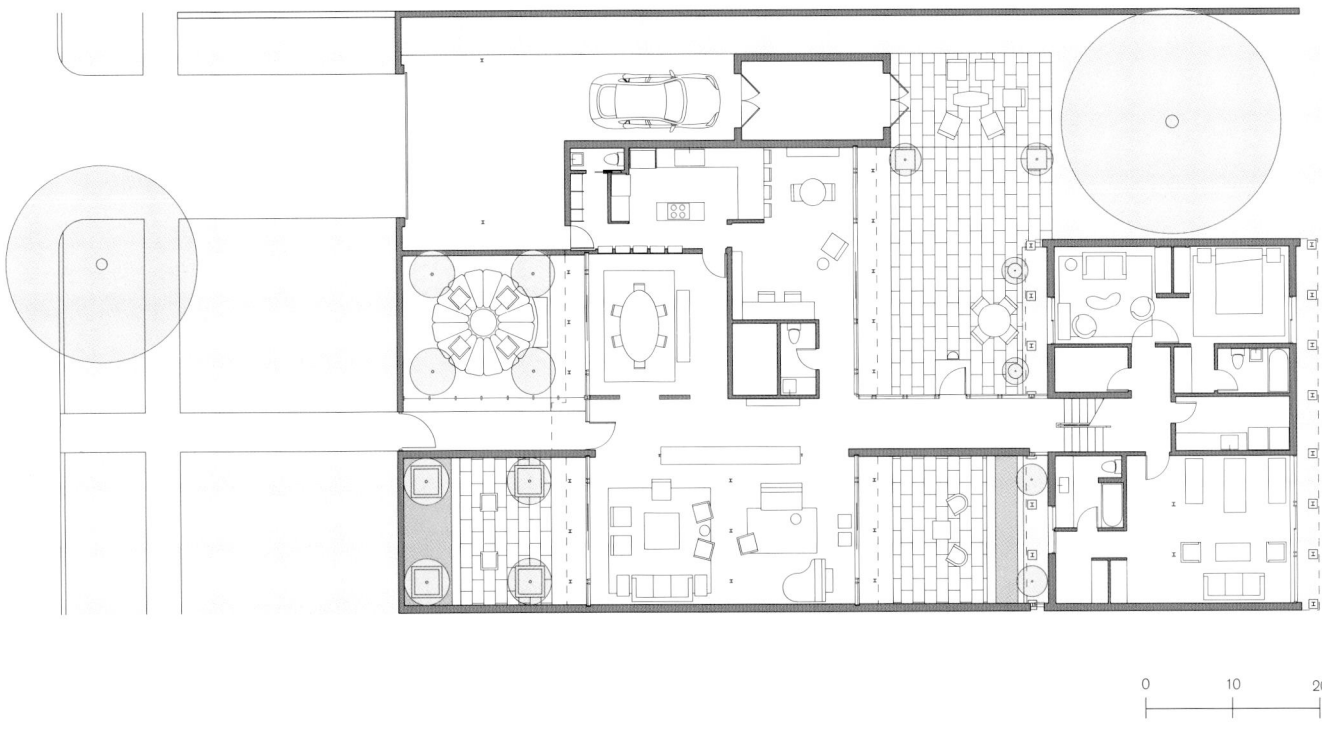

ABOVE Floor plans. OPPOSITE A vintage Khotan carpet and antique Louis XVI bench sit below a marble shelf original to the entry hall of the residence.

ABOVE Ceramic sculptures by Eva Hild and Peter Lane share the dining room with a large photograph by Jungjin Lee and Napoleon III chairs. OPPOSITE Black river stones and native hollies highlight the original flower-shape design of the dining room courtyard.

ABOVE The kitchen was updated with white quartz countertops and grass cloth that complement the existing walnut millwork. **OPPOSITE** Vintage Ion chairs by Gideon Kramer in blue and a Scissor chair by Pierre Jeanneret upholstered in saffron yellow add color to the breakfast room.

A nineteenth-century Oushak carpet anchors an eclectic mix of modern and antique chairs in the living room.

ABOVE In the hallway, George Nelson–designed wood and glass display cases house a ceramics collection. The early-twentieth-century totem pole is original to the house. **RIGHT** Sculptural chairs by Rodolfo Bonetto from the 1970s sit among topiaries, hollies, and palms in the living-room courtyard.

ABOVE In the master bedroom, vintage brass stools by Milo Baughman are upholstered in Fortuny fabric while the George Nelson headboard, original to the house, is clad in yellow mohair. OPPOSITE A Jack Pierson photograph, a French bergère, and a Khotan carpet adorn the new master bath in the location of a former bedroom.

ABOVE AND OPPOSITE A new guest suite with sitting room and bedroom was created from combined and reconfigured children's bedrooms. Furnishings include swivel chairs by William Haines and a sofa by Paul Frankl. An Alex Harris photograph hangs above the custom bed.

BAYOU BONFOUCA

SLIDELL, LOUISIANA

Designed for artist George Dunbar, this house is a wholly contemporary interpretation of the vernacular architecture indigenous to southern Louisiana. Occupying the high end of a peninsula where a bayou and a canal intersect, the home has seemingly limitless views across the water to protected marshlands. An artesian pond meanders through a grove of live oak trees and beds of native lilies and elephant ears, separating the new house from an existing artist's studio. In the near distance, egrets and herons alight on the briny water, and bands of nutrias—a mainstay of Louisiana's once fabled fur industry—paddle from shore to shore. The site is pure magic.

Tall yet compact, the one-story house is composed of a large living/dining room framed by a master suite to the left, a kitchen and study to the right, and a large gallery facing the bayou. Stylistically, the design has roots in the steep-roofed Creole houses that dominated farms and plantations before the Civil War. But this is no nostalgic riff on antebellum architecture. The design details are abstracted versions of relevant archetypes, distilled to accentuate purity of line and form while responding to the contours of the landscape. The pitch of the roof, for example, was purposely exaggerated to give the structure a heightened presence within the miles-long sprawl of bayou wilderness.

The materials palette is limited to travertine, stucco, painted brick, wood, and plaster. The standing-seam metal roof is beige, while the interiors are largely off-white—all the better to appreciate the artwork on display. As for furnishings, the eclectic assemblage encompasses country French family heirlooms and chic steel-frame furniture that Dunbar himself designed in the 1950s. At 2,500 square feet, the residence is relatively modest in size, but the soaring 20-foot ceiling gives the effect of a much larger space; that feeling is reinforced by the wall of glass addressing the sweeping wetlands. The expansive scheme is punctuated by the vanishing edge of the lap pool, where spring-fed water spills over a retaining wall and merges with the bayou beyond.

PREVIOUS PAGES The residence seen at dusk from the bayou.
OPPOSITE The owners' antiques, including a stone sculpture and painted Italian side chair, occupy the curved entry vestibule.
FOLLOWING PAGES A gravel driveway framed by live oaks draped in Spanish moss leads up a gentle knoll to the residence.

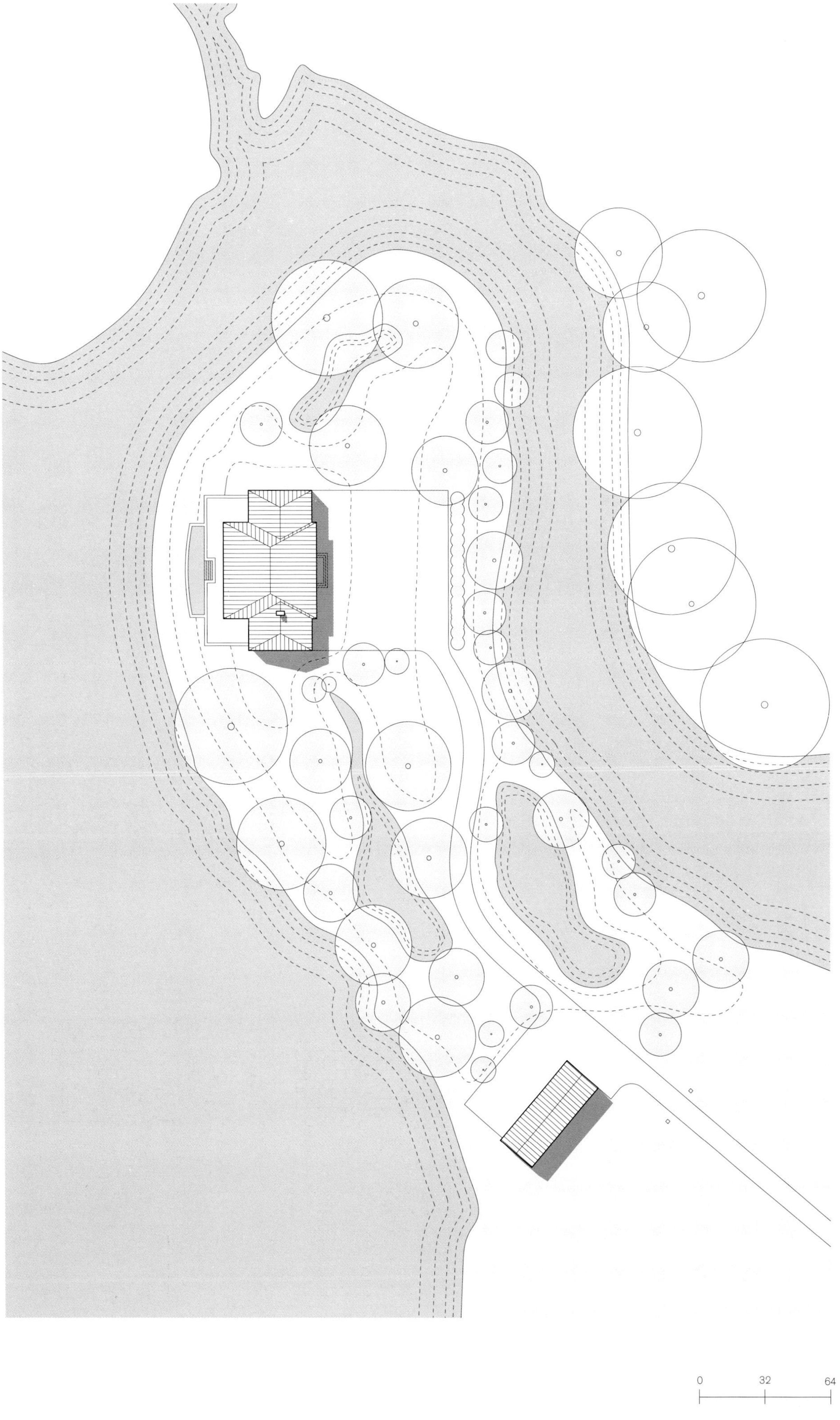

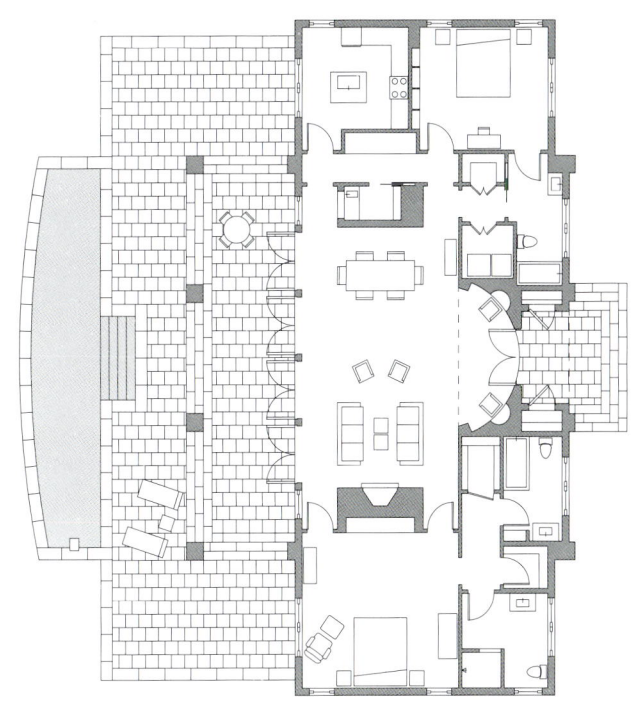

ABOVE Entry facade with large, shuttered windows, pilasters, and translucent glass doors. **RIGHT** Floor plan. **OPPOSITE** Site plan. **FOLLOWING PAGES** Aerial view of living/dining room with travertine floors and tall French doors.

PREVIOUS PAGES A George Dunbar painting hangs above the fireplace, which was adapted from a colonial stone entryway purchased in Mexico. **ABOVE** The master bedroom, containing artworks by Dunbar and Franz Kline, is wrapped with windows that offer views of the bayou. **OPPOSITE** A charcoal drawing by Dunbar's daughter hangs above a French commode. **FOLLOWING PAGES** The curved lap pool is fed by an artesian spring.

BOXWOOD COURT
MONROE, LOUISIANA

Over the course of more than two decades, a multiphased renovation of this 1920s English-cottage-style brick house effectively expanded the structure's footprint and flow to accommodate the clients' growing family and ever-expanding art collection. One of the fundamental mandates of the project was the desire to foster a more intimate connection between the house's interior rooms and its outdoor entertaining areas and garden. Another objective was to broker an easy rapprochement between the traditional bones of the house and the modern spirit of the family—as well as their collection of modern and contemporary art.

As the house's footprint expanded, the kitchen became its center—the intersection of the three main wings and the primary route to the courtyard in back, which was designed by landscape architects Sawyer/Berson to function as an outdoor double parlor. In the latest renovation, accomplished after the children were grown, the kitchen was transformed into a social space that accommodates art, reinforces the view from the formal entry hall to the courtyard, and provides comfortable seating. The cabinets and walls are paneled with cerused oak reminiscent of a study, and most of the appliances are concealed below Basaltina stone countertops.

The formal living room, anchored by a custom sofa and coffee table, reads as timeless and classic. The color palette is decidedly neutral, in contrast to the polychromatic den, which is outfitted in vintage mid-century furnishings by Edward Wormley and Pierre Paulin. The bright blues of the den reappear in the husband's office, a wonderland of rare baseball collectibles. Upstairs, the classic and the contemporary once again mingle amicably. The serene master suite is accented with quiet notes of pale blue, while a guest bedroom sports a felicitous wallpaper pattern of wild banana-leaf palms.

PREVIOUS PAGES A boldly striped Edward Wormley sofa, a custom coffee table, and Pierre Paulin lounge chairs are anchored by a reproduction Ingrid Dessau flat-weave carpet. **OPPOSITE** A Sol LeWitt painting hangs above a Charlotte Perriand swivel chair.

LEFT In the entry hall, paintings by Milton Avery and John Alexander commingle with a Frank Fleming sculpture atop a Ledbetter-designed Lucite console.
FOLLOWING PAGES An antique Baccarat chandelier hangs in the dining room. The vintage dining chairs are by Harvey Probber, and the artworks are by John Marin, David Bates, Milton Avery (in hallway), and Joan Mitchell.

PREVIOUS PAGES In the living room, an antique Oushak carpet sits beneath a custom sofa, cast glass coffee table, and lounge chairs by Harvey Probber. Artworks include a self-portrait by Chuck Close, a George Dunbar painting, and a ceramic sculpture by Pamela Sunday. **ABOVE** The husband's study is outfitted with a collection of vintage baseball memorabilia. The chairs are by T. H. Robsjohn-Gibbings and Edward Wormley, and the vintage desk is by Harvey Probber. **OPPOSITE** Banana-leaf wallpaper and 1950s rattan monkeys share the guest room with a David Bates self-portrait.

ABOVE In the master bedroom, watercolors by Milton Avery hang above a custom bed with built-in side tables and a custom leather-wrapped television cabinet. **OPPOSITE** The master dressing room, outfitted with padded leather closet doors, contains artworks by Emil Bisttram and Charles Burchfield. An antique Dutch chandelier hangs above the walnut island.

79

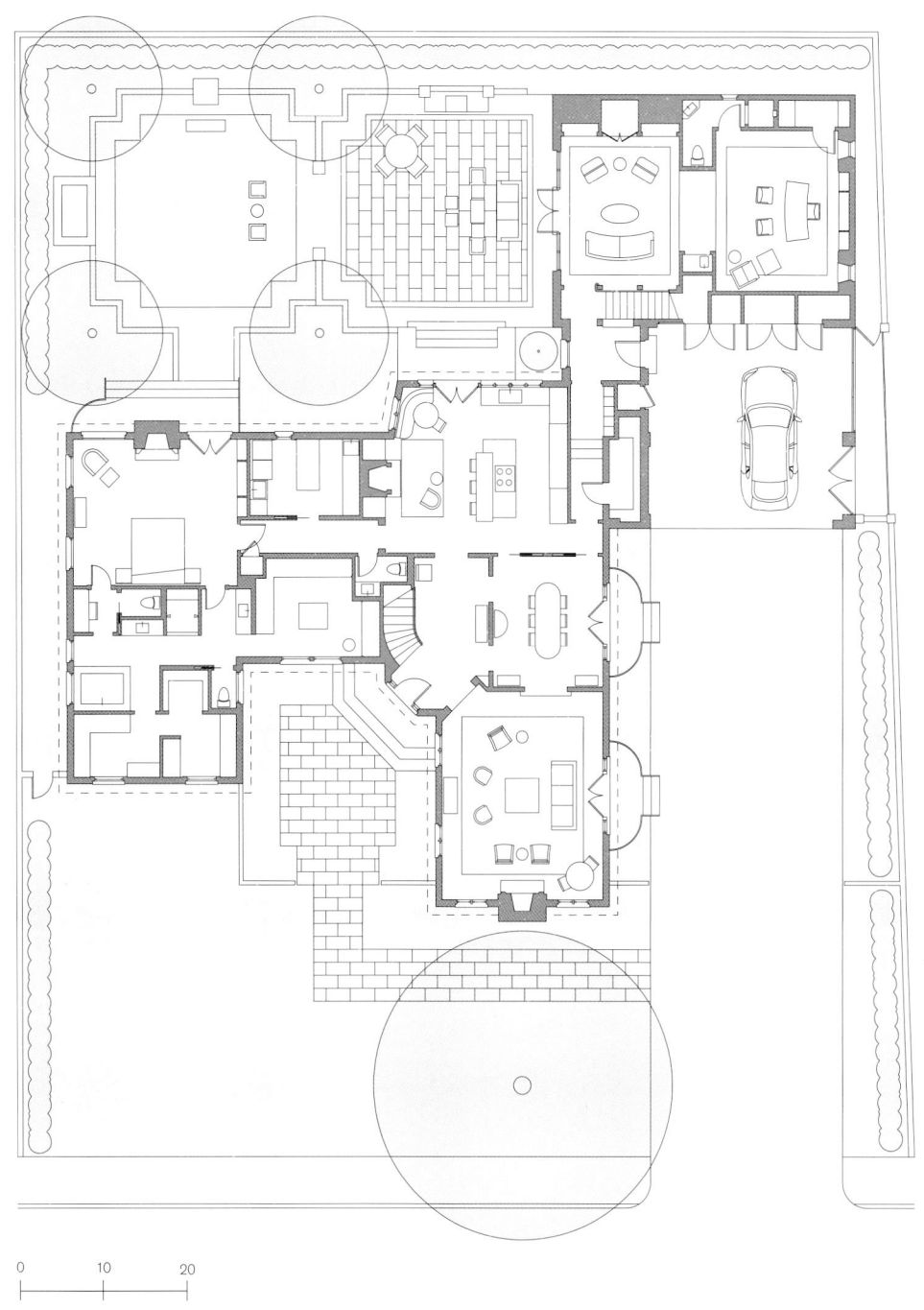

0 10 20

ABOVE Site/floor plan. **OPPOSITE** Ledbetter's addition takes its design cues from the house's original English cottage style and frames a garden designed by landscape architects Sawyer/Berson. **FOLLOWING PAGES** The kitchen is paneled in cerused oak with a Basaltina stone fireplace and countertops. A custom banquette shares the seating area with a Dorothy Schindele side chair, Paul Tuttle bar stools, and an Adrian Pearsall swivel chair. The painting is by David Bates.

This house occupies a hilltop on the south side of Avery Island, Louisiana, a place synonymous with the McIlhenny Company and its signature product, Tabasco pepper sauce, which has been produced here since 1868. The homeowners, fifth-generation members of the McIlhenny family, had long admired Thomas Jefferson's architecture, particularly his Palladian plantation house Poplar Forest in Virginia. This structure nods to Palladio with a formal, cross-axial plan. But since Avery Island is a community of casual second homes and weekend houses, the exterior detailing and fenestration are decidedly more regional than classical, completely at ease among its vernacular neighbors.

Like Poplar Forest, the plan is organized around a central square, but in this case the square evolves volumetrically into a perfect cube that contains a freestanding octagonal dining room. The dining room has double walls that conceal a stair that leads to a widow's walk on the south side of the house, facing Vermilion Bay and the Gulf of Mexico. The dramatic southern vista is framed by an existing allée of mature live oaks. The house's open plan, organized around the focal square, takes maximum advantage of panoramic, 360-degree views. Except for the master bedroom, the spaces are all painted a warm white, accentuating the clerestory light that pours into the octagonal dining room and filters out to the adjacent living spaces.

The decorative scheme encompasses a mix of family heirlooms, furnishings and accessories collected by the homeowners on their travels, and newly added pieces selected to consolidate the centuries-spanning ensemble into a cohesive whole. French Directoire antiques and Asian artworks rub shoulders happily with American mid-century modern designs by the likes of Paul Frankl and T. H. Robsjohn-Gibbings. The potentially disparate grouping is unified by a muted palette of fabrics in beige, brown, and pale blue. Strategic decorative elements—most notably the 1960s Italian Murano chandeliers that crown the entrance hall and the 35-foot-high central dining room— enliven the overall atmosphere of restraint and order.

PREVIOUS PAGES The house sits atop a hill that it shares with ancient live oaks and native palmettos. **OPPOSITE** Assorted objects from the owners' collection of Chinese pottery.

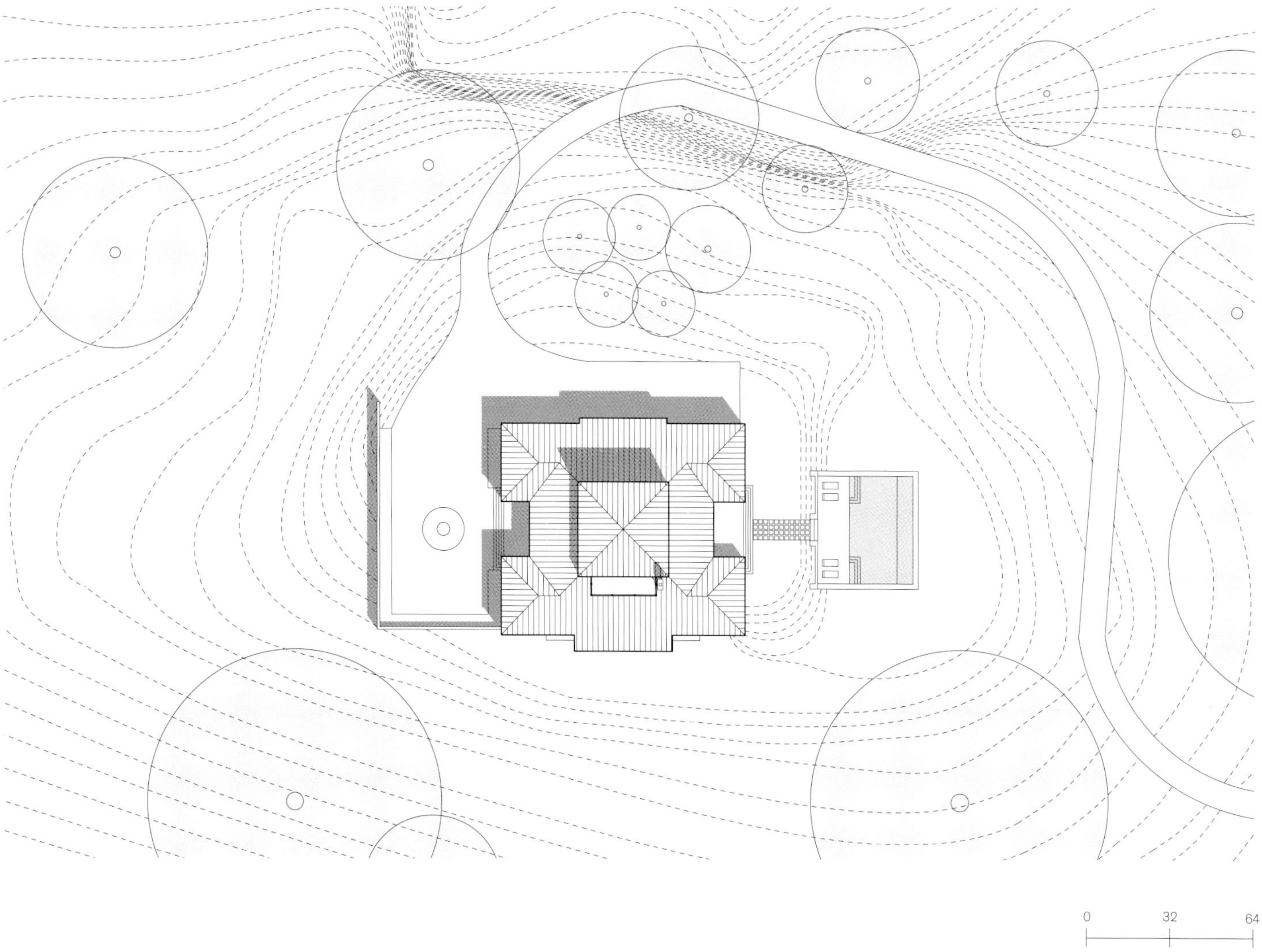

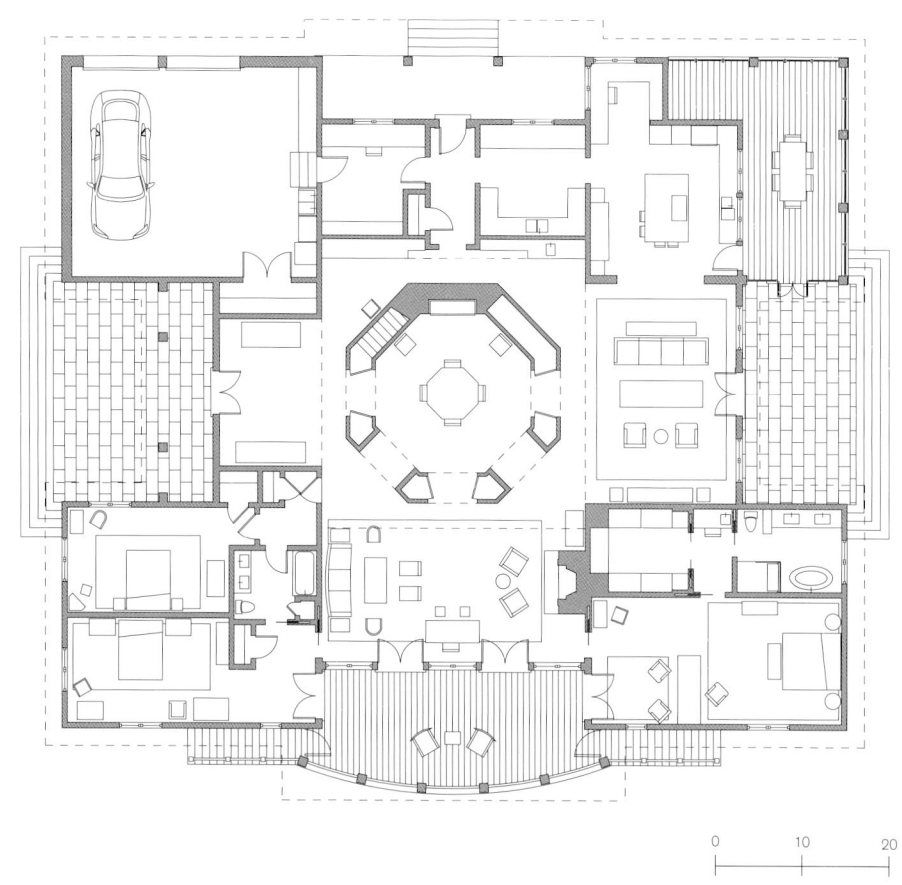

ABOVE Site plan. RIGHT Floor plan.
OPPOSITE An impressive 1960s Murano chandelier hangs within the octagonal, double-height dining room.
FOLLOWING PAGES The octagonal dining room sits within a larger cube of space in the center of the house.

ABOVE In the entry hall, a Peter Lane ceramic platter sits atop a massive, vintage T. H. Robsjohn-Gibbings low table once owned by the wife's grandmother. **OPPOSITE** The dining room's double walls conceal a staircase that leads to a widow's walk.

ABOVE Clerestory windows bring natural light into the dining room and adjacent areas below. OPPOSITE In the master bedroom, bedside tables fashioned from antique pepper barrels support vintage mirrored, trapezoidal lamps and a faux tortoise headboard, also from the grandmother's estate. FOLLOWING PAGES An eclectic mix of French and English antiques and Edward Wormley slipper chairs gather in the living room. The south-facing wall of continuous French doors and transoms opens to a deep porch.

ABOVE The kitchen is clad with custom bamboo cabinets and opens to a screened dining porch. **RIGHT** The curved, south-facing porch offers views to pepper fields at the base of the property and to Vermilion Bay beyond. **FOLLOWING PAGES** The swimming pool occupies a grass parterre on the east side of the house.

BAYOU DESIARD
MONROE, LOUISIANA

Drawing inspiration from raised plantation cottages, this house incorporates a wide center hall and an outdoor gallery within an asymmetrical composition that responds to the site configuration and opportunities for sweeping views. The site is a promontory where two bayous intersect; more than half of its perimeter is formed by water. From one angle, the house faces a golf course across the bayou. In the opposite direction, the residence faces an uninterrupted vista two miles upriver.

Embracing nature in a meaningful way was the key to the site plan. Bayou DeSiard laps up to serpentine wooden boardwalks that wrap the property. Mature bald cypress trees stand knee-deep in the water, dripping Spanish moss. Like the intersecting waterways, the rooms of the house flow easily from one to the next, eliminating the need for formal hallways. Nodding to northern Louisiana plantation antecedents, the dwelling is only a single story high. The design, however, is hardly an exercise in orthodox historicism, as evidenced by its idiosyncratic architectural details and absence of shutters.

A formal columned portico stands at the center of a broad gable at the front of the house. At the client's request, the brick facade is painted in pale yellow—specifically, a shade replicated from the historic Beauregard-Keyes House in New Orleans. Inside, an imposing entry hall culminates in a barrel-vaulted living room with a 22-foot-high ceiling. Looking out to the bayou, a covered porch at the rear of the house, visible through French doors and transoms, provides an eminently gracious gathering place for the family.

The interiors combine bespoke upholstered furniture with a mix of pedigreed antiques. The walls and rugs are mostly beiges and blues. Custom-designed chandeliers temper the scale of the living room, where subtly colored silk window treatments and textured linen fabrics echo the gentle palette of a Chinese needlepoint carpet.

PREVIOUS PAGES A broad gable, a portico, and generous steps define the entry to the residence.
OPPOSITE A Sawyer/Berson-designed, 600-foot-long, serpentine boardwalk hugs the water's edge.

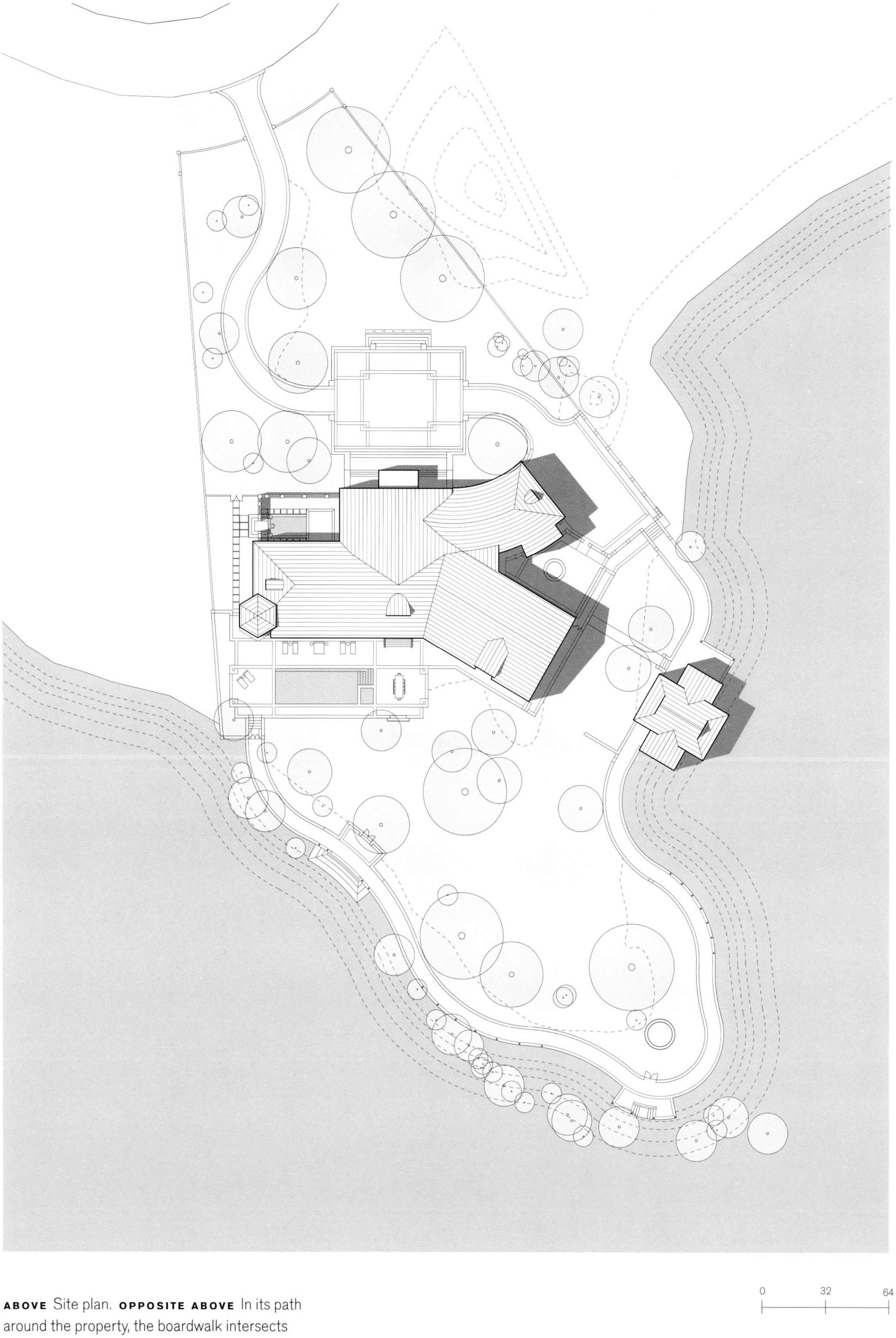

ABOVE Site plan. **OPPOSITE ABOVE** In its path around the property, the boardwalk intersects large decks, water steps, a hammock, and, here, the boathouse. **OPPOSITE BELOW** Floor plan.

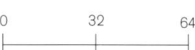

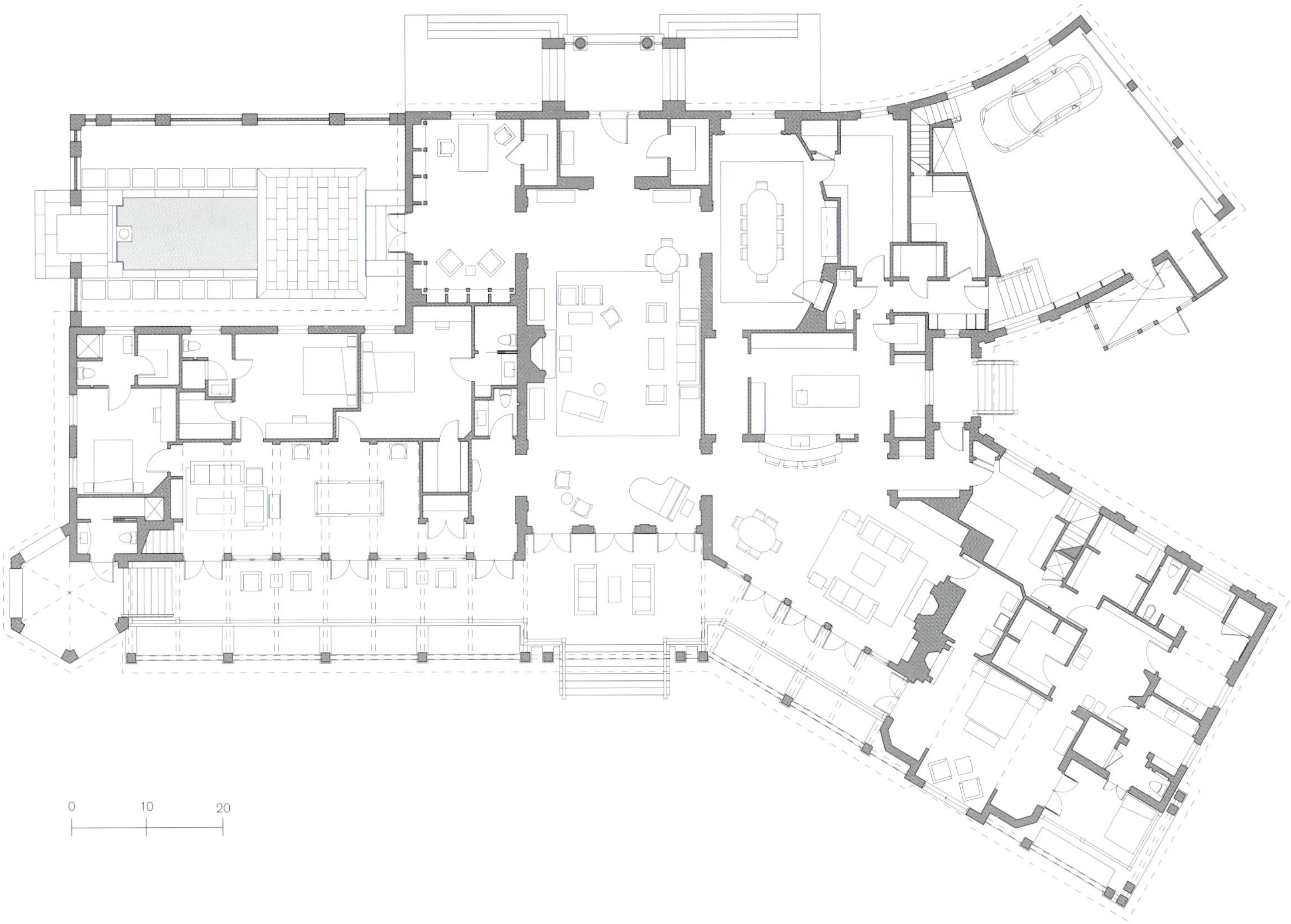

0 10 20

ABOVE The study's herringbone-pattern leather floor tiles echo the mahogany tones of the wood paneling and bookshelves. **OPPOSITE** Elaborate millwork ennobles the entry hall.

ABOVE A Jacqueline Humphries painting commands a seating area with a vintage Baker coffee table. **RIGHT** Pale gray painted and waxed wood paneling adorns the walls in the barrel-vaulted living room.

ABOVE A Terry Winters print rests on the fireplace mantel, and French doors lead to a covered porch. **OPPOSITE** In the master bedroom, a tall window invites views of the intersecting bayous and cypress trees. **FOLLOWING PAGES** The roof of the back porch extends well beyond the stone terrace, protecting family and friends from Louisiana's harsh sun and heavy rains.

DECATUR STREET
FRENCH QUARTER, NEW ORLEANS

Hinting at its past life, this 2,400-square-foot, two-story loft in a nineteenth-century industrial building was converted into an upscale residential apartment with views of the historic French Market and the Mississippi River. Existing ceilings of rough-hewn timber were maintained throughout, as were selected areas of plaster-skimmed exposed-brick walls. The original wide-plank heart pine floors were also salvaged, adding another layer to the warm, highly textured space.

A new kitchen was conceived as a white insert within the otherwise wood-toned ensemble. Its existing brick wall was painted white to reflect natural light from windows on adjacent and opposite walls. A white Corian-clad island was designed around existing wood columns to provide a casual seating space for the kitchen and to establish a subtle delineation between the kitchen and living area.

Large vintage Murano chandeliers hang from the beamed ceilings in the living room, accompanied by vintage Murano table lamps in the two primary seating areas. The furnishings consist of mid-century modern classics by T. H. Robsjohn-Gibbings, Edward Wormley, and Harvey Probber. The color palette of orange and green was chosen to complement the rich browns of the architecture. A large sisal carpet grounds the furniture arrangements and, like the white-painted brick wall, lightens the room.

Upstairs, the master bedroom's brick walls were painted white and softened with white linen curtains to create a serene refuge. A custom bed and vintage Gilbert Rohde side tables and desk extend the largely neutral palette, while a persimmon-colored vintage lounge chair and orange lizard-skin lamps by Karl Springer pick up the vibrant color accents from the floor below. A new stair with a Hollywood Regency–inspired painted steel railing was inserted to connect the two floors and enliven the entry hall.

PREVIOUS PAGES The living room, dining room, and kitchen share a large open space in the renovated warehouse building. Chandeliers and lamps are vintage Murano. **OPPOSITE** A Rocio Rodriguez painting and vintage Edward Wormley and T. H. Robsjohn-Gibbings chairs define one of the seating areas.

ABOVE Fretwork-patterned carpet complements a new brass and painted steel stair railing. **LEFT** The strong geometry of parallel wood beams is echoed in the artwork, curtains, and chair back. **FOLLOWING PAGES** Vintage Karl Springer lamps flank a custom bed in the master bedroom. The painting is by John Patrick Salisbury.

EAST END AVENUE
NEW YORK CITY

The owners of this residence purchased two apartments overlooking Carl Schurz Park and Gracie Mansion in a new luxury building on Manhattan's Upper East Side. The challenge was to combine the units into a cohesive 3,500-square-foot apartment with a gracious arrangement of living spaces while conforming to existing locations of structural, electrical, and mechanical systems. Major rooms—living, dining, and master suite—were located on the east and south facades to take advantage of views of the park and the East River. A core of mechanical systems and storage spaces floats within the living room to accommodate an entertainment center, pantry, wet bar, silver closet, and service corridor. At the same time, the service core conceals structural columns and delineates seating areas within the living room.

The large east- and south-facing living/dining room feels very much like a well-lit loft. Furnishings and fabrics were carefully selected to unify the space without distracting from the striking views. The owners came to the project with a love for mid-century modern furnishings and contemporary art, so it seemed natural to endow the apartment with the feeling of a pristine, white-box gallery.

Italian antiques share space with American and French modern furniture as well as Ledbetter-designed sofas, tables, and beds. Vintage light fixtures by Charles Hollis Jones and Gaetano Sciolari sparkle within the rooms, while sculptural ceramic pieces by Eva Hild, Peter Lane, and Pamela Sunday sit comfortably alongside collections of art glass.

PREVIOUS PAGES Artworks by Eva Hild and Nancy Lorenz share space with a custom tessellated-horn console and antique Jacques Adnet chairs. **OPPOSITE** A Charles Hollis Jones pendant fixture hangs above linen-covered dining chairs by Maurice Bailey for Monteverdi-Young. The ceramic planters are by Peter Lane.

ABOVE A custom walnut and brass console and sectional sofa define a seating area adjacent to the dining room. **OPPOSITE** The living room ensemble includes a Ledbetter-designed sofa and coffee table, antique Murano lamps, vintage Edward Wormley side tables, and Harvey Probber lounge chairs. The gueridon is by Hervé Van der Straeten.

The master bedroom is furnished with Peter Lane ceramic lamps and faceted tables, a vintage Eames chaise, Chinese carpets, and a painting by Margaret Evangeline.

LAKE PONTCHARTRAIN

LAKE TERRACE, NEW ORLEANS

Lean yet muscular, this residence was specifically designed to house a cutting-edge collection of contemporary paintings and photography, including works by Cindy Sherman, Alex Katz, Pat Steir, Sam Taylor-Wood, Gregory Crewdson, Collier Schorr, and Jacqueline Humphries. With the exception of a double-height, north-facing glass curtain wall, the massing of the house is solid and planar, limiting the damaging effects of natural light on the photography. The entry is signaled by the garage volume pulling away from the main body of the house, a feature that also allows for a sitting terrace with views of Lake Pontchartrain above the garage roof.

The exterior of the house—a minimalist composition of rectangular volumes articulated in silver-gray brick—approximates the sober beauty of a classic white-box art gallery. But within the home, the individual rooms are detailed to convey a softness and intimacy better suited to residential life. A sculptural, serpentine staircase, framed within the glass curtain wall, connects the lower and upper levels of the house, throwing an emphatic curve into the rectilinear scheme. An arched, floating ceiling plane similarly tempers the scale and rigid lines of the voluminous living room. An interior spine clad in warm white oak serves as a foil to the house's cool white plaster walls and black slate floors.

The decorating here matches the architecture in confidence and complexity. Rather than capitulating to the contemporary artworks with an all-modern scheme of furnishings, the mix embraces a broad range of Louis XVI, Biedermeier, Empire, and twentieth-century designs. Louis XVI–style chairs cozy up to a classic modern dining table by Florence Knoll beneath a vintage brass Gino Sarfatti chandelier in the dining room, while Poul Kjaerholm's Danish modern lounge chairs face off against patent leather English fauteuils in the living room. The result of these ministrations is a house that ennobles the estimable artworks on view as well as the quotidian rituals of home life.

PREVIOUS PAGES The facade is composed of rectangular brick volumes interrupted by a large, double-height window that showcases the sculptural curved staircase. **OPPOSITE** A Cindy Sherman photograph graces a double-height, white-oak-paneled wall that separates the entry area from the living room and garden beyond.

PREVIOUS PAGES A Tina Barney photograph hangs above a custom sofa in the study. The French armchairs are signed Jacob, and the vintage side tables are by Edith Norton. **RIGHT** A curved plaster ceiling floats above the living room. The owner's collection includes photographs by James Casebere, Nan Goldin, Adam Fuss, Robert Mapplethorpe, and others.

ABOVE A Thomas Struth photograph hangs above a console by Eliel Saarinen and a giltwood stool in the living room. **RIGHT** A Jacob side chair sits behind a custom cerused teak-and-goatskin desk adjacent to an Alex Katz painting.

ABOVE In the dining room, a Gregory Crewdson photograph faces a vintage Florence Knoll table and Louis XVI–style side chairs. The vintage brass chandelier is by Gino Sarfatti.
OPPOSITE A Pat Steir painting and a Biedermeier bench adorn a freestanding wall that separates the living and dining rooms. An Alex Katz cutout sculpture peers in from the far corner.

ABOVE Large Baccarat pieces share the wet bar counter with a photograph by Collier Schorr.
OPPOSITE A vintage Mazzega Murano chandelier hovers above a Warren Platner table in the breakfast room. The painting is by Emily Eveleth.

ABOVE A photograph by Herb Ritts anchors the end wall of the travertine-clad master bath. **RIGHT** The master bedroom looks out to a park dotted with live oaks. The photograph is by Sam Taylor-Wood.

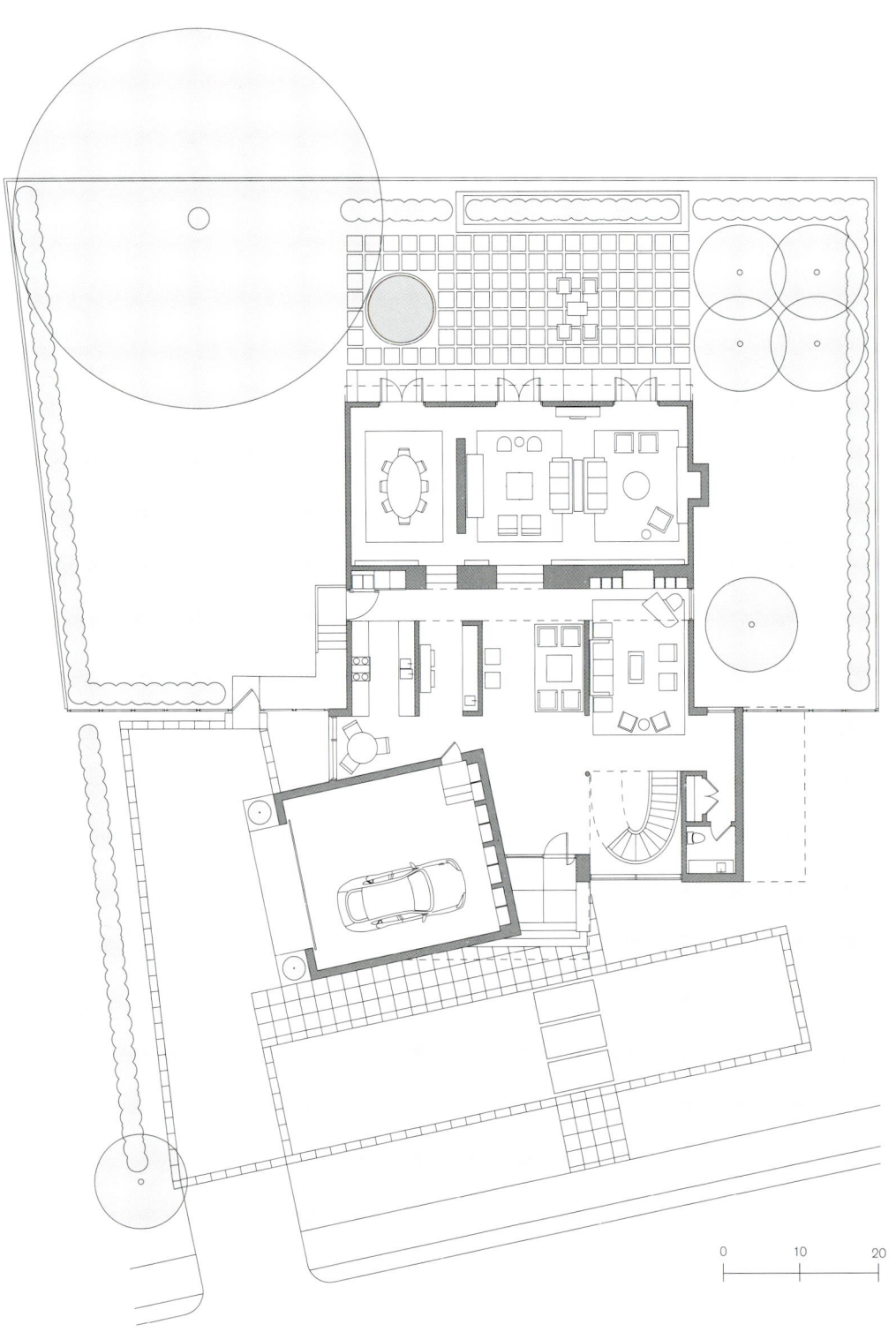

ABOVE Site/floor plan. **RIGHT** At night, the house glows like a lantern as the large windows provide glimpses of the art and furnishings within.

ESPLANADE AVENUE
FAUBOURG MARIGNY, NEW ORLEANS

Situated in the Faubourg Marigny, this 1829 Greek Revival house had been divided up into apartments before its recent transformation back to a single-family dwelling. The romantic patina of the weathered pink stucco facade belies the startlingly mod sensibility that animates the interiors. This is a house that gathers inspiration from the past while wholeheartedly embracing the present. One of the major moves in the extensive renovation was the expansion of existing 3-foot-wide doorways between rooms to 8 feet, enhancing spatial flow, opening views, and facilitating the influx of natural light. Existing crown moldings and baseboards were replicated to preserve the rooms' historic integrity. The dramatic black-and-white color scheme underscores the venerable structure's good bones and generous proportions.

The home's contemporary ethos is expressed in a broad array of twentieth-century modern furnishings. Eschewing predictable signifiers of mid-century cool, the scheme incorporates elements of wide-ranging pedigree and provenance, including works by Osvaldo Borsani, Warren Platner, and contemporary French maestro Hervé Van der Straeten. Judiciously selected eighteenth- and nineteenth-century antiques tether the home to its historic past—indeed, several mirrors are original to the property. In contrast, the living and dining rooms' giant keyhole-shaped mirrors in the Surrealist manner of French designer Serge Roche strike a decidedly more modern note.

Every sofa is custom-designed, including the living room's 13-foot sectional, which is covered in a silk velvet whose color wavers intriguingly between gunmetal and bronze. Other furnishings and finishes leaven the severity of the black-and-white palette by introducing sympathetic shades of brown, gray, and glints of gold. The wide-plank pine floors were stained in a custom color—70 percent ebony, 30 percent coffee-brown—and topped off with three coats of high-gloss polyurethane for a patent-leather luster. The three-room master bedroom suite, bathed in white and redolent of Old Hollywood glamour, feels like a dreamy aerie, at once timeless and of the moment.

PREVIOUS PAGES In the second-floor master suite, antique Maison Baguès chandeliers and Regency-style giltwood mirrors complement a custom curved sofa, vintage Jan Ekselius chairs, and a vintage T. H. Robsjohn-Gibbings coffee table.
OPPOSITE Much effort went into preserving the patina of the exterior stucco, the shutters, and the trim colors.

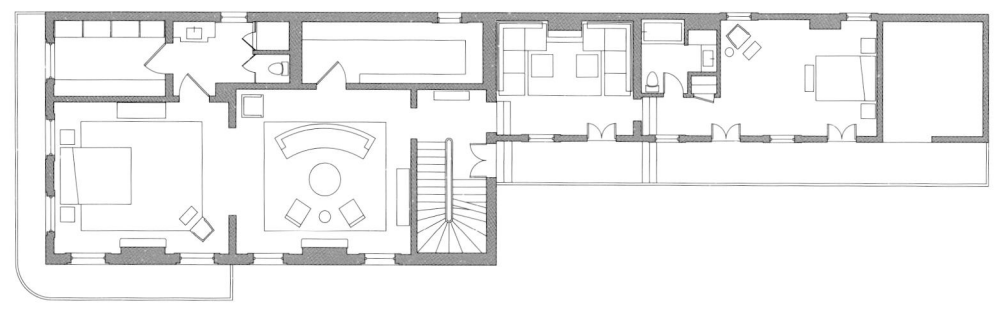

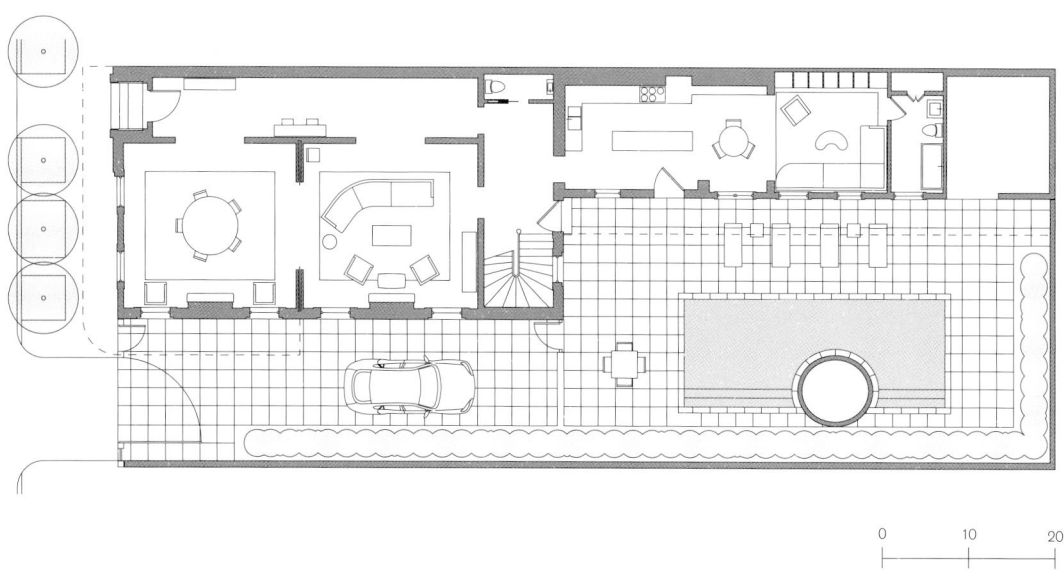

ABOVE Floor plans. **OPPOSITE** Artworks by Dawn DeDeaux, Pablo Atchugarry, and Mitchell Lonas inhabit the stair hall.

ABOVE A swimming pool was designed around a nineteenth-century cistern that now houses the pool equipment. **OPPOSITE** In the kitchen, a Warren Platner table and vintage Osvaldo Borsani chairs sit adjacent to French doors that lead into the courtyard. **FOLLOWING PAGES** The kitchen den is furnished with a custom sectional sofa, a 1950s French chandelier, Fortuny pillows, and a Moroccan area rug. The painting is by George Dunbar.

ABOVE In the living room, a large custom curved sofa upholstered in silk velvet sits across from bergères by Maison Jansen. The bronze pendant and occasional table are by Hervé Van der Straeten.
OPPOSITE Ledbetter designed the brass-and-granite dining table surrounded by Louis XVI–style side chairs of mahogany, gilt, and horsehair, by Maison Jansen. The artwork is by Robert Gordy.

Massive ceramic lamps by Peter Lane frame a custom bed. The balcony overlooks Esplanade Avenue.

In the guest room, a vintage Murano snowflake chandelier and period giltwood French mantel mirror pop against charcoal gray striae wallpaper.

CHESTNUT STREET
GARDEN DISTRICT, NEW ORLEANS

Lee Ledbetter and Associates was engaged to provide interior design services for a 3,000-square-foot house constructed in the 1850s on a charming side street in the Garden District of New Orleans. The firm collaborated with Bell Architects to combine rooms by removing existing walls and fireplaces, and to devise custom millwork, new bathrooms, and a kitchen. In the decorating sphere, Ledbetter designed custom furniture and carpets to complement classic modern pieces by Paul McCobb, Edward Wormley, and T. H. Robsjohn-Gibbings, as well as the homeowners' collection of vintage modern Brazilian furniture.

On the main level, two original parlors were conjoined into one large living/dining room to facilitate entertaining. Modern chandeliers discreetly define individual areas within the open expanse. Custom plaster medallions above the chandeliers were inspired by historic properties in New Orleans. The furniture is a mix of mid-century modern and antiques, along with bespoke sofas. The dominant colors are gray-green and persimmon.

The rooms to the back of the house have a more casual, club-like feel, with an abundance of pattern on pattern in rich browns, coppers, and blue-greens. A peacock-blue banquette runs the length of the breakfast room; the color extends into the adjacent den in the mohair on a bespoke sofa. Custom bookcases, with *verre églomisé* panels framed in brass, occupy the north wall.

Upstairs, the study is covered in dark brown cork wallcovering with a gold background that glints from behind the cork as it catches the light. The ceiling is covered in gold leaf. A more serene palette prevails in the master bedroom, which imports cool blues in the form of wool curtains and a vintage Venini glass chandelier. The tone reemerges in the navy-blue wainscot and cabinetry of the new master bath.

PREVIOUS PAGES Paintings by Regina Scully and Mark Beard face off in the large living/dining room.
OPPOSITE The Greek Revival sidehall residence occupies a quiet Garden District side street.

A large custom angular sofa sits adjacent to painted French fauteuils and a T. H. Robsjohn-Gibbings lounge chair.

ABOVE The gold leaf ceiling in the second floor study echoes the gold background of the dark brown cork wallpaper. The chandelier is by Pierre Le Royer.
OPPOSITE A massive nineteenth-century giltwood mirror and contemporary brass sconces from France form the backdrop for a Lindsey Adelman chandelier, a Matthew Hilton dining table, and vintage Baker walnut chairs.

PREVIOUS PAGES In the den, custom *verre églomisé* panels reflect natural light from the adjacent garden. Edward Wormley swivel chairs and Harvey Probber bolster chairs flank a custom mohair sofa. **ABOVE** The breakfast room and den share chocolate-brown-and-white wallpaper, ikat linen window treatments, matching custom carpets, and peacock blue seating. **OPPOSITE** The cabinets and tile backsplash extend the teal blue palette into the kitchen. In the breakfast room, a print by an unknown Cuban artist hangs above a vintage Brazilian bar cabinet.

ABOVE In the master bedroom, a Venini chandelier and artwork by Marcel Ceuppens hang above the custom bed, headboard, and end tables. The gunmetal-glazed ceramic lamps are by Pamela Sunday. **OPPOSITE** The blue theme continues in the wall tile and cabinets of the master bath. The stool is vintage Baker.

SACKETT STREET
HOUSTON, TEXAS

A young Houston attorney with a passion for modern architecture purchased a circa 1980 home designed by Marvin Watson, Jr., on the edge of the Greenway neighborhood and engaged Lee Ledbetter and Associates to undertake a significant architectural renovation and new interior design. The primary architectural change involved removing as many interior walls as possible to usher natural light through the house and simultaneously offer broader, more gracious areas for entertaining. The strategy is perhaps most evident in the reconfigured relationship between the long entry hall and the adjacent living room. Once discrete, the two zones are now connected by three generous openings; the center opening houses a glass display case for the owner's collection of antique toy soldiers. Additionally, the kitchen, bathrooms, and fireplaces were all updated, and an outdoor pool cabana was fully enclosed to function as a den/wet bar.

A touchstone for the decor was the celebrated American fashion maestro Halston, whose taste for minimal, modern interiors with a dash of decadence exerted nearly as much influence as his clothing. Most of the rooms in this house adhere to a palette of neutral gray, which comes to life with particular drama in the living room's 30-foot-long sectional sofa covered in luxurious mohair. On the upper floor, a former bedroom was transformed into a study swathed in chocolate brown walls that recall the color of the brick floors on the lower level; accents of acid green, yellow, and red nod to an antique Oushak carpet that grounds the room. Throughout the home, Ledbetter-designed custom pieces rub shoulders with classic pieces by Mies van der Rohe, Harvey Probber, Mario Bellini, Milo Baughman, and Cedric Hartman.

PREVIOUS PAGES Mitchell Lonas nest paintings and a gray mohair sectional sofa face tables by Nicos Zographos and swivel chairs by Harvey Probber. **OPPOSITE** Outdoor furniture by Richard Schultz and a monumental Peter Lane ceramic vessel occupy a covered porch between the swimming pool and the large living room.

Mirrored end walls accentuate the length of the large living room. An artwork by James Drake is installed above a new limestone fireplace.

Uniform gray carpet, upholstery, and curtains envelope the space while the white-painted trusses and ceiling seem to hover above.

PREVIOUS PAGES Ledbetter connected the entry hall to the adjacent living room with two large openings that flank a new glazed display case for the owner's collection of antique lead soldiers. **ABOVE** The kitchen was refreshed with new furnishings, including a vintage Reggiani chandelier and vintage Pace Collection bar stools. **OPPOSITE** Detail of the display case.

ABOVE A James Kennedy painting hangs above a custom bed. The 1970s side tables consist of open smoked-glass cubes above closed stainless-steel cubes. **OPPOSITE** A seating area at the foot of the bed is anchored by a new limestone fireplace, paintings by Duilio Barnabe, and cantilevered stainless-steel chairs by Milo Baughman.

ABOVE The dining room doubles as a library. A Serge Mouille chandelier hangs above a custom mohair banquette, a marble table, and Mies van der Rohe–designed Brno chairs. The painting is by Helge Hommes. **OPPOSITE** In the pool room, a Julie Blackmon photograph overlooks a vintage Pace Collection coffee table and Mario Bellini lounge chairs.

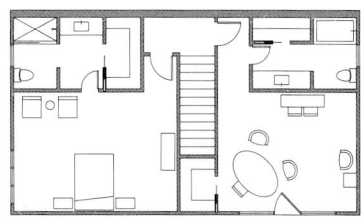

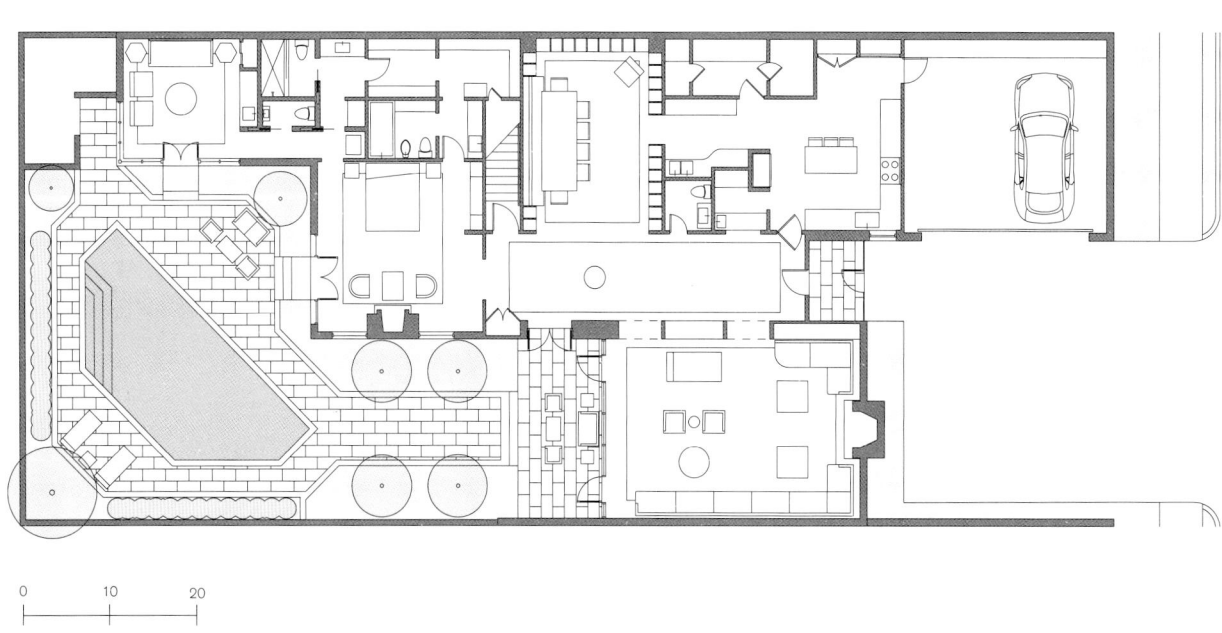

0   10   20

ABOVE Floor plans. **OPPOSITE** In the home office, classic modern pieces by Florence Knoll, Charles and Ray Eames, and Warren Platner sit atop a vintage Oushak carpet. An artwork by Russell Prince hangs on chocolate-brown-painted walls.

FISK-HOPKINS HOUSE
FRENCH QUARTER, NEW ORLEANS

This house was originally constructed in the late 1850s as a single-story Greek Revival library and billiard room for an adjacent home. The pavilion was sold in 1871 and converted into a proper residence with the addition of a second story and an Italianate cast-iron balcony. Ledbetter worked closely with his client to adapt the striking five-bay residence for modern living. While plaster crown moldings and elaborate door and window casings were painstakingly restored, walls were removed to create large spaces that showcase the building's wraparound windows, a rare attribute in the French Quarter. Similarly, the curving staircase, previously hidden within a small, elevated vestibule, was brought to the ground, opened to the public rooms, and redesigned to appear free-floating.

A new kitchen and sitting area replaced a warren of service spaces, and the second floor was redesigned to accommodate master and guest suites. Anthemion-crested cornices, which had been added to the living room's French doors in the late nineteenth century, were repurposed as window cornices in the master bedroom, an area formerly devoid of crown molding. A new master bathroom centers on existing French doors and a small balcony. Its floors and walls are swathed in the same boldly veined Italian marble from which the bespoke bathtub was carved.

The landscape design features symmetrical hollies and palm trees, planes of green lawn, bluestone pavers, and a large flush-edged swimming pool. The crisp, orderly arrangement echoes the carefully edited interior design of white walls, gray fumed-oak floors, white and gray fabrics, and plush seating. Modern furniture, art, and light fixtures stand in sharp contrast to the original historic envelope but remain connected through color, scale, and abundant natural light.

PREVIOUS PAGES An interior wall was removed to open the capacious living room to the adjacent study and staircase. **OPPOSITE** The Fisk-Hopkins residence as seen through date palms across a new swimming pool.

New fumed-oak herringbone floors, a ceiling medallion, and a Louis XVI–style mantel complement French doors, plaster crown moldings, and an eighteenth-century giltwood mirror original to the house.

ABOVE The kitchen is outfitted with white glass and nickel-framed cabinet doors that reflect light from nearby windows. The room shares a deep plaster cove with the adjoining den. **OPPOSITE** A painting by Anastasia Pelias hangs above a custom white marble mantel adjacent to the owner's collection of photographs of New Orleans jazz legends. The chandelier is vintage Murano, and the swivel chairs are by Milo Baughman.

ABOVE A white pendant by Stephen Antonson hangs from a new skylight within a plaster cove in the stair hall. **OPPOSITE** Walls below and in front of the staircase were eliminated to create a free-floating effect and to open the stair to the living room. The custom runner is wool and silk, and the painted bronze sculpture is by Joseph Havel.

In the dining room, vintage chairs by Vladimir Kagan, upholstered in python-printed leather, surround a custom dining table in faceted, white-painted steel and stone. The sculpture is by George Dunbar.

In the sitting area of the master bedroom, a photograph by Jungjin Lee rests atop a custom mantel. The bespoke white chaises are joined by a wood sculpture by Dawn DeDeaux.

PREVIOUS PAGES A custom bed and end tables share the master bedroom with vintage Baker slipper chairs, a Stephen Antonson plaster pedestal table, and vintage Osvaldo Borsani side chairs. The paintings are by George Dunbar and Dawn DeDeaux. **ABOVE** From inside the house, the facade's Italianate cast-iron columns and arches frame views to the swimming pool. **OPPOSITE** An antique French chandelier hangs above the master bath, where the floors, walls, counters, and tub were fabricated from dramatically veined Italian marble.

JOAN MITCHELL CENTER
ESPLANADE RIDGE, NEW ORLEANS

Soon after Hurricane Katrina, the New York City–based Joan Mitchell Foundation commissioned a state-of-the-art studio building for a newly established visiting artists' residency program in New Orleans. The Joan Mitchell Center occupies a large, open space in the middle of a residential block in the Esplanade Ridge Historic District, an eighteenth- and nineteenth-century neighborhood. The center's 8,000-square-foot studio building, certified LEED Gold for its sustainability initiatives, hugs two perimeter edges of its unusual mid-block site. The L-shaped structure frames a large outdoor green space, effectively creating a campus quad that connects the main administrative building to these new artists' studios. With sloped roofs and clapboard siding, the studio building defers to the neighborhood's historic homes in scale, materials, and architectural character. Accessed from a pedestrian bridge that traverses a new bioswale, the building contains ten artist studios, a common room, a digital technology lab, and support spaces.

The double-height studios are individually articulated, with skylights and large north-facing monitors. This configuration provides ideal conditions for artists' work, reducing the need for artificial illumination and minimizing direct light. A louvered screen element, designed to mitigate Louisiana's harsh western light, defines the border between the studios and the outdoor common space. The lawn is gently sloped to direct storm water to the bioswale and retention pond, providing necessary relief for the city's strained drainage system. Lee Ledbetter and Associates collaborated with landscape architects and a native plant specialist to create a natural setting designed to attract local birds and insects, with little need for irrigation after planting.

PREVIOUS PAGES North-facing light monitors capture natural light for individual studios and act as lanterns at night. **OPPOSITE** Skylights, clerestory windows, and supplemental perimeter fixtures provide the studio spaces with maximum flexibility for color rendering with light.

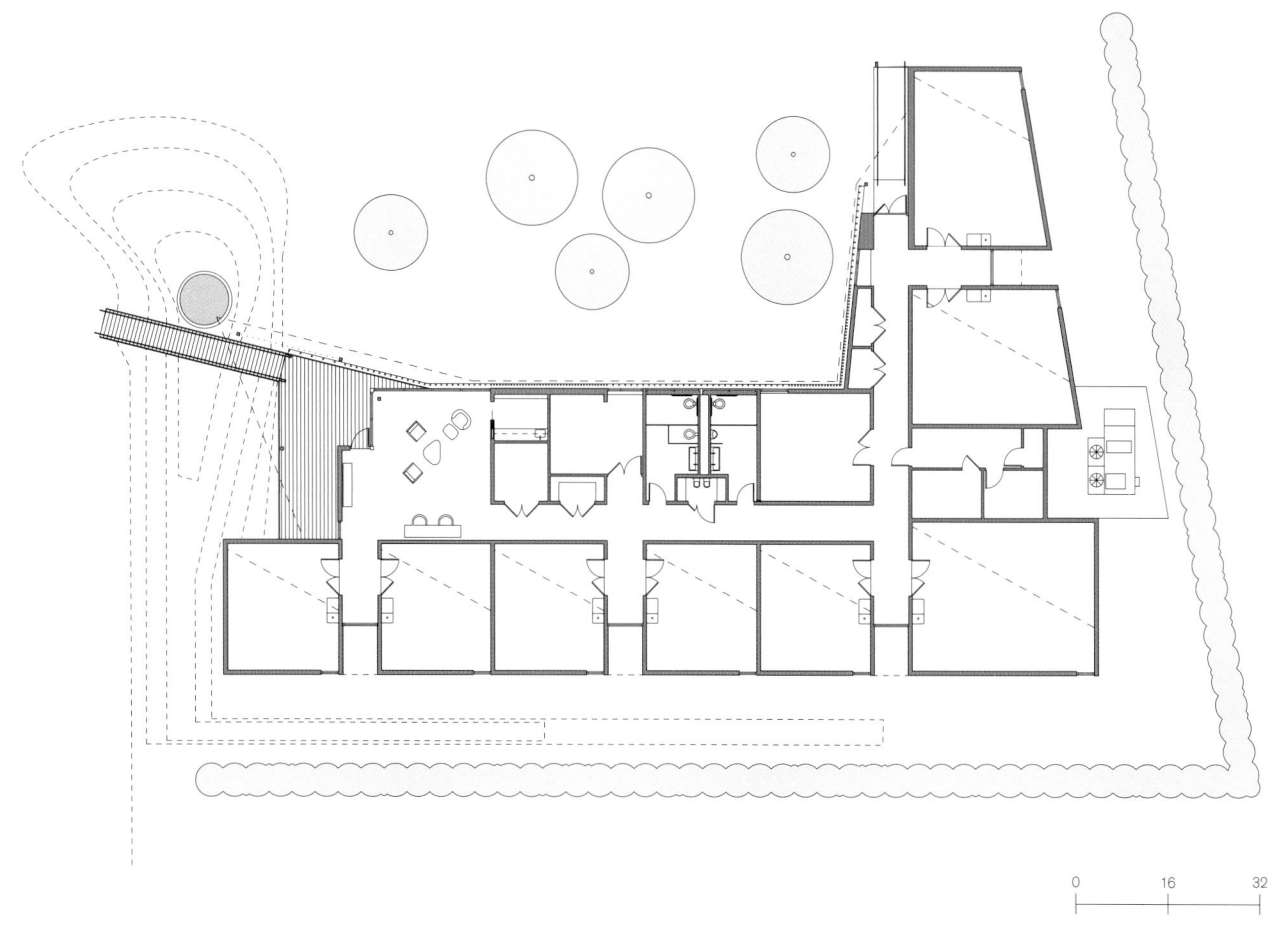
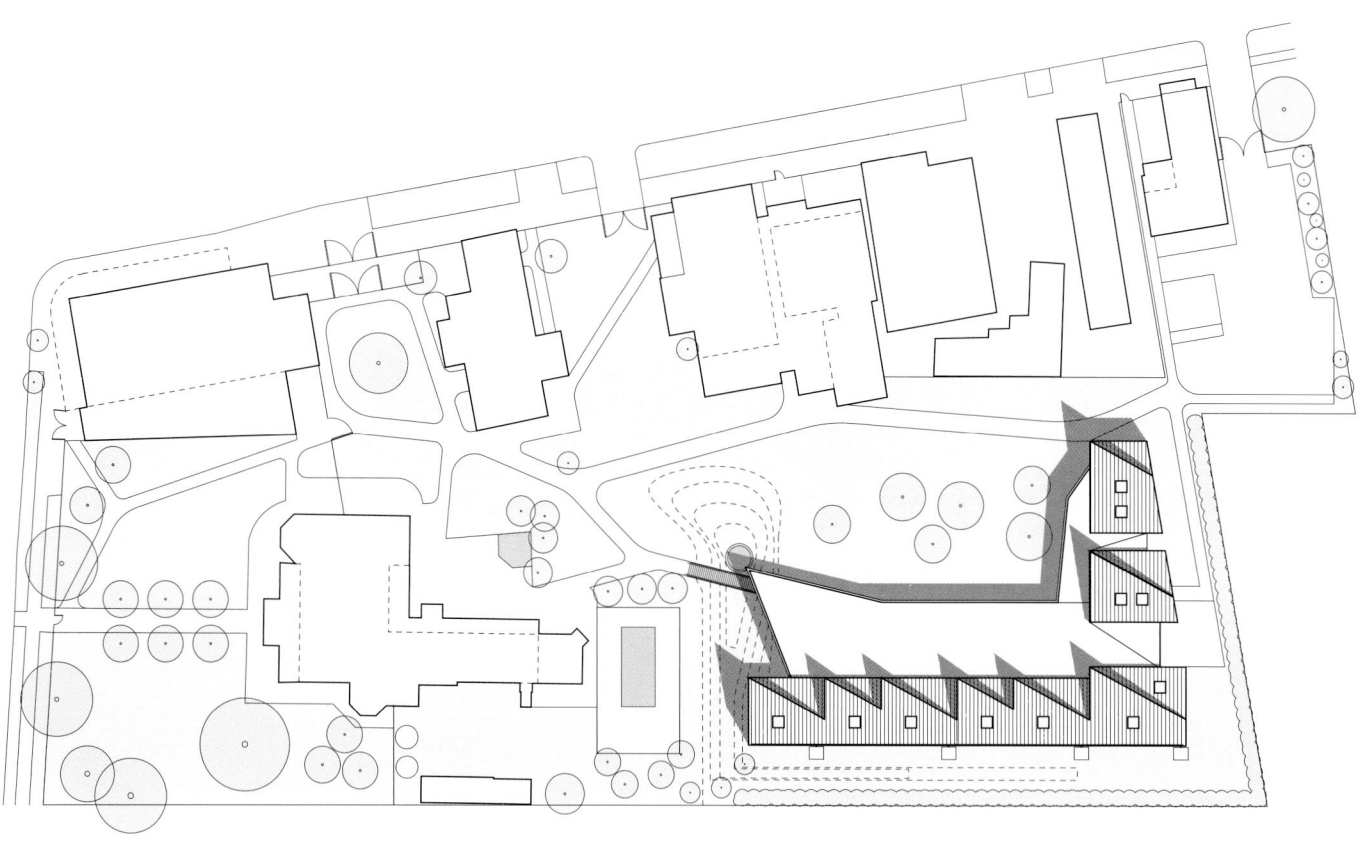

ABOVE The artists' common room looks out at the large campus lawn. A portrait of Joan Mitchell in her studio serves as inspiration. OPPOSITE ABOVE Floor plan. OPPOSITE BELOW Site plan. FOLLOWING PAGES On the approach to the studio building's main entry, a bridge crosses a bioswale integral to the water management system.

Looking to the future of its congregation, the St. Charles Avenue Presbyterian Church commissioned Lee Ledbetter and Associates to renovate most of the church's ground-floor level, excluding the main sanctuary. The project accomplished multiple goals: the conversion of an existing chapel into a library and reading room; the creation of a new chapel with greater seating capacity than its predecessor; and the design of an outdoor columbarium—an above-ground structure with niches to hold crematory urns—in a garden adjacent to the original sanctuary.

The historicist modernism of architect Eliel Saarinen's Cranbrook Academy of Art provided inspiration for the design scheme, which also takes cues from the existing Neo-Gothic sanctuary's architectural details. Oak paneling, pilasters, and coffered ceilings within the new spaces create a common design language that unifies the historic and the contemporary. In the new chapel, an arced ceiling form, designed in response to height restrictions, gently promotes a mood of spiritual uplift, while specially commissioned stained-glass windows by Louisiana artist Stephen Wilson employ vivid colors to depict the creation story from Genesis.

The siting of the columbarium garden next to the historic sanctuary echoes the relationship of medieval cloisters to Gothic cathedrals. Designed as a walled garden, with stonework derived from the original church architecture, the columbarium contains a triple-pedestal fountain that symbolizes the Trinity. The sound of running water has the additional benefit of muffling nearby street noise. A hundred-year-old live oak shades the sanctified garden.

PREVIOUS PAGES A new oak-paneled chapel with a gently vaulted ceiling replaced former classrooms. The stained glass windows are by Louisiana artist Stephen Wilson. **OPPOSITE** Bronze-clad walls in the columbarium are interrupted by small openings to the surrounding landscape.

Languid live oak limbs act as a ceiling above the columbarium garden. The architects designed the triple-pedestal fountain.

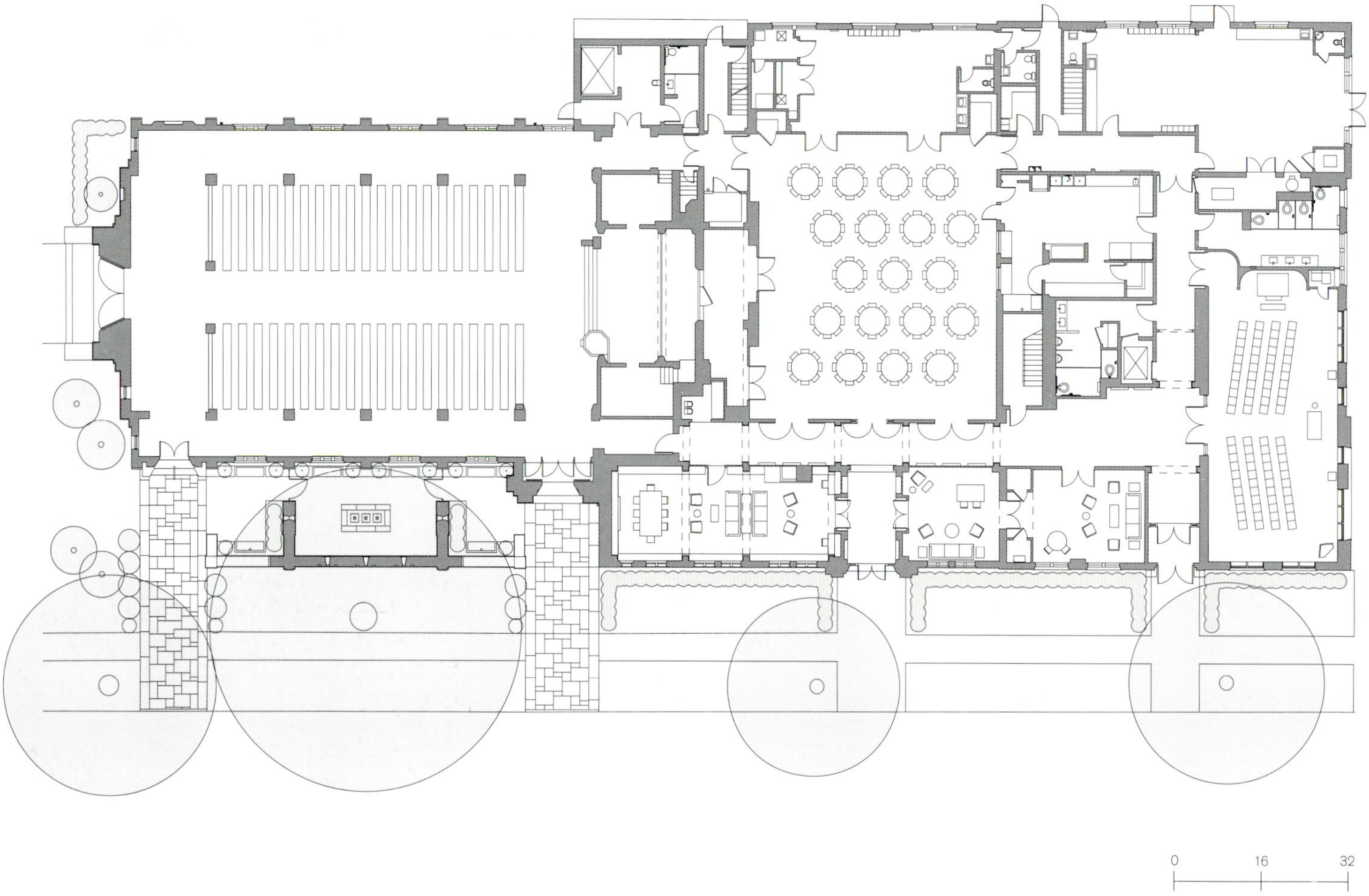

ABOVE Entrance to new chapel.
OPPOSITE ABOVE The columbarium is sympathetic to the original Neo-Gothic-style sanctuary in materials and architectural details.
OPPOSITE BELOW Floor plan.

SYDNEY AND WALDA BESTHOFF SCULPTURE GARDEN

NEW ORLEANS MUSEUM OF ART, CITY PARK

This sculpture garden occupies five acres in City Park adjacent to the New Orleans Museum of Art. A lagoon bisects the picturesque site, creating two distinct halves. The garden, designed in collaboration with New York City–based landscape architects Sawyer/Berson, accommodates sixty outdoor sculptures in a layout where visual connections are in most cases implied rather than dictated. The site is organized around a central axis that runs from the paired entry pavilions to a secondary entrance near the City Park Botanical Garden. Depending on the location, this axis is either clearly defined by paths or expressed solely as a view corridor.

The abstracted geometries of the garden's architectural features create a quiet backdrop for a collection comprised of both figurative and abstract sculptures by Henry Moore, Barbara Hepworth, Antoine Bourdelle, Jacques Lipchitz, Aristide Maillol, George Segal, Louise Bourgeois, Anish Kapoor, George Rickey, and others. The placement of those outstanding sculptures beneath centuries-old live oaks and within groves of mature pine trees elucidates the garden's special character.

The entry pavilions, bridges, gates, niches, and terraces are consistently detailed in cast stone, bronze, and stainless steel, materials shared with the adjacent museum building. At the lagoon's edges, grading was gently manipulated to allow three pedestrian bridges to remain discreet and flat, seamlessly woven into the fabric of the land.

PREVIOUS PAGES In a secondary garden entrance, bronze-and-stainless-steel gates open to a sculpture by Gaston Lachaise. **OPPOSITE** Fernando Botero's *Mother and Child* stands within a cathedral of live oaks.

ABOVE The oak grove with a sculpture by Joel Shapiro. OPPOSITE A monumental sculpture by Kenneth Snelson occupies the lagoon.

RIGHT *Figure with Tear and Arrow* by Sandro Chia appears to recline in deference to one of Louise Bourgeois's iconic bronze spiders, while a site-specific glass sculpture by Jean-Michel Othoniel hangs from a tree limb. **FOLLOWING PAGES** Two pavilions and the main entry gates flank Henry Moore's *Reclining Mother and Child*.

CREDITS

PROJECTS

DUMAINE STREET: Original Architect: Unknown; Renovation Architect: Lee Ledbetter Architects; Architect-in-Charge: Lee Ledbetter; Assistant Architect: Scott Evans; Interior Designer: Lee Ledbetter; Landscape Architect: Luis Guevara Landscape Services

MARQUETTE STREET: Original Architect: Nathaniel "Buster" Curtis, Curtis & Davis; Renovation Architect: Lee Ledbetter & Associates; Architect-in-Charge: Lee Ledbetter; Assistant Architect: Amy Petersen; Interior Designer: Lee Ledbetter; Landscape Architects: Luis Guevara Landscape Services, NOLA + Design Inc.

BAYOU BONFOUCA: Original Architect: Lee Ledbetter Architects; Architect-in-Charge: Lee Ledbetter; Assistant Architects: Richard Fullerton, Karri Maggio, Robert Riccardi; Landscape Architect: Owner; Structural Engineer: Robert A. Bouchon, Zehner & Bouchon Consulting Engineers Inc.

BOXWOOD COURT: Original Architect: Unknown; earlier renovation by William Mattison; Renovation Architect: Lee Ledbetter & Associates; Architect-in-Charge: Lee Ledbetter; Assistant Architects: Chris Loudon, Amy Petersen, William Soniat Jr., Michael Sewell; Interior Designers: Lee Ledbetter, Susan Boyd, Lee Lormand; Landscape Architect: Sawyer/Berson

CHERRY HILL: Original Architect: Lee Ledbetter Architects; Architect-in-Charge: Richard Fullerton; Assistant Architects: Tarra Cotterman, Scott Evans, Jarod Moninger; Interior Designers: Lee Ledbetter, Susan Boyd; Structural Engineer: Robert A. Bouchon Consulting Engineer LLC

BAYOU DESIARD: Original Architect: Lee Ledbetter Architects; Architect-in-Charge: Lee Ledbetter; Assistant Architects: Richard Fullerton, Robert Riccardi, Karri Maggio, Scott Evans. Interior Designers: Lee Ledbetter, Lyle LeBlanc; Landscape Architect: Sawyer/Berson; Lighting Designer: Cline Bettridge Bernstein Lighting Design; Structural Engineer: Datum Architects/Engineers Inc.

DECATUR STREET: Original Architect: Lee Ledbetter Architects; Architect-in-Charge: Lee Ledbetter; Assistant Architect: Richard Fullerton; Interior Designers: Lee Ledbetter, Lee Lormand, Susan Boyd; Landscape Architect: Luis Guevara Landscape Services

EAST END AVENUE: Original Architect: Ledbetter Fullerton Architects; Architects-in-Charge: Lee Ledbetter, Richard Fullerton; Assistant Architects: Curtis Laub, Tarra Cotterman, Chris Loudon, Justin Agnew; Interior Designers: Lee Ledbetter, Susan Boyd, Amy Petersen, Tyson Geary

LAKE PONTCHARTRAIN: Original Architect: Lee Ledbetter Architects; Architect-in-Charge: Scott Evans; Assistant Architects: Richard Fullerton, Marty McElveen, Karri Maggio; Interior Designers: Lee Ledbetter, Lee Lormand, Lyle LeBlanc; Landscape Architect: Luis Guevara Landscape Services; Lighting Designer: Davis Mackiernan Architectural Lighting; Structural Engineer: Robert A. Bouchon Consulting Engineer LLC

ESPLANADE AVENUE: Original Architect: Unknown; Renovation Architect: Ledbetter Fullerton Architects; Architect-in-Charge: Tarra Cotterman; Assistant Architects: Richard Fullerton, Curtis Laub, Chris Loudon; Interior Designers: Lee Ledbetter, Susan Boyd, Zeke Jordan III; Landscape Architect: Luis Guevara Landscape Services

CHESTNUT STREET: Renovation Architect: Bell Architecture; Interior Designers: Lee Ledbetter, Tarra Cotterman; Landscape Architect: Luis Guevara Landscape Services, NOLA + Design Inc.; Structural Engineer: Walter Zehner & Associates

SACKETT STREET: Original Architect: Marvin Watson Jr., Minzenmayer/McGee Associate Architects; Renovation Architect: Lee Ledbetter & Associates; Architect-in-Charge: Amy Petersen; Interior Designers: Lee Ledbetter, Amy Petersen; Landscape Architect: Fajkus & Company Landscape Architects and Contractors

FISK-HOPKINS: Original Architect: Unknown; Renovation Architect: Lee Ledbetter & Associates; Architects-in-Charge: Lee Ledbetter, Chris Loudon; Assistant Architects: Curtis Laub, Tarra Cotterman, Kim Payne Allen; Interior Designers: Lee Ledbetter, Paul Zansler; Landscape Architect: NOLA + Design Inc.; Structural Engineer: Anderson Engineers Inc.

JOAN MITCHELL CENTER: Original Architect: Lee Ledbetter & Associates; Architect-in-Charge: Tarra Cotterman; Assistant Architects: William Soniat Jr., Peter Kilgust, Will Rosenthal, Amy Petersen; Landscape Architects: Luis Guevara Landscape Services, Evans + Lighter Landscape Architecture; Lighting Designer: Star Lighting Design; Structural Engineer: Avegno Bailey & Associates; MEP Engineer: Lucien T. Vivien Jr. & Associates

ST. CHARLES AVENUE PRESBYTERIAN CHURCH: Original Architect: W. W. Van Meter with early renovations by The Mathes Group; Renovation Architect: Lee Ledbetter & Associates; Architect-in-Charge: Amy Petersen; Assistant Architect: Tarra Cotterman; Landscape Architects: Luis Guevara Landscape Services, Landscape Images Ltd.; Lighting Designer: Cline Bettridge Bernstein Lighting Design; Structural Engineer: Avegno Bailey & Associates; MEP Engineer: Lucien T. Vivien Jr. & Associates

SYDNEY AND WALDA BESTHOFF SCULPTURE GARDEN: Original Architect: Lee Ledbetter Architects; Architects-in-Charge: Lee Ledbetter, Richard Fullerton; Assistant Architects: Karri Maggio, Scott Evans, Lyle LeBlanc, Caroline Kwong, Nichole Chauvin, Michael Diodati; Landscape Architect: Sawyer/Berson; Lighting Designer: Cline Bettridge Bernstein Lighting Design; Structural Engineer: Burk-Kleinpeter Inc.; MEP Engineer: Huseman Wang Inc.

PHOTOGRAPHERS

PETER AARON/OTTO: 102–3, 104, 107, 108, 109, 114–15
STEVEN BROOKE for *Architectural Digest*/Condé Nast: 16, 50–51
PAUL COSTELLO: 52, 54–55, 57, 58–59, 60-61, 62, 63, 64–65, 240
PIETER ESTERSOHN: endpapers, 8, 10, 84–85, 86, 90–91, 92, 93, 94, 95, 96–97, 98, 99, 100–101, 124–25, 126, 128, 129, 130–31, 164–65, 166, 168–69, 170, 171, 172–73, 174, 175, 176, 177, 178–79, 180, 182, 183, 184–85, 186, 187, 188, 189, 190, 191, 193, 194–95, 196, 198–99, 200, 201, 202, 203, 204, 205, 206–7, 208, 209; Pieter Estersohn for *Architectural Digest*/Condé Nast: 6–7, 12, 32–33, 34, 37, 38, 39, 40, 41, 42–43, 45, 46, 47, 48, 49, 150–51, 152, 155, 156, 157, 158–59, 160, 161, 162, 163; Pieter Estersohn for *Elle Decor*: 238; Pieter Estersohn for *Galerie*: 15, 66–67, 68, 70–71, 72–73, 74–75, 76, 77, 78, 79, 81, 82–83
TIMOTHY HURSLEY: 210–11, 212, 215, 216–17, 218–19, 220, 222–23, 224, 225
HENRIK A KNUDSEN JR.: 44
MICHAEL LUPPINO for *Traditional Home*: 110, 111, 112, 113
MICHAEL MUNDY for *House & Garden*: 18–19, 20, 22–23, 24, 25, 26, 27, 28, 29, 30, 31
PATRICK SALISBURY: 89, 116–17, 118, 120, 121, 122–23
JASON SCHMIDT for *House & Garden*: 4, 134, 136–37, 138–39, 140, 141, 142, 143, 144, 145, 147, 148–49
RICHARD SEXTON: 132–33, 146, 226–27, 228, 231, 232–33; *Untitled (Burton: "Right Angle Chairs"/Graham: "Source Figure")*, The New Orleans Museum of Art: Museum purchase, Besthoff Sculpture Garden Fund, 2004.160.10: 2–3; *Untitled (Shapiro: "Untitled")*, The New Orleans Museum of Art: Museum purchase, Besthoff Sculpture Garden Fund, 2004.160.5: 230; *Untitled (Entrance gates, evening)*, The New Orleans Museum of Art: Museum purchase, Besthoff Sculpture Garden Fund, 2004.160.17: 234–35

SOURCES

PAGES 124–31: Jacques Adnet chairs, Carol Egan bench, and Hervé Van der Straeten table courtesy Maison Gerard, New York; vintage European glass and ceramics courtesy The End of History, New York; selected ceramic tables, tray, and planters courtesy Peter Lane Clay, Brooklyn, New York; antique pillows courtesy Antique Textiles Collection, New York; paintings in dining room and master bedroom courtesy Margaret Evangeline, Brooklyn, New York; antique carpets in master bedroom courtesy Nazmiyal Antique Rugs, New York.

PAGES 194–209: David Borgerding sculpture and George Dunbar sculpture and painting courtesy Callan Contemporary, New Orleans; Anastasia Pelias painting courtesy Jonathan Ferrara Gallery, New Orleans; Dawn DeDeaux sculpture courtesy the artist; Dawn DeDeaux painting and Joseph Havel sculpture courtesy Arthur Roger Gallery, New Orleans; Kevin Gillentine ceramics courtesy Kevin Gillentine Gallery, New Orleans; Karen Gundlach ceramics courtesy the artist; selected vases, urns, throw pillows, and accessories courtesy Dunn and Sonnier, New Orleans; Paola Paronetto vases, selected white vases, vintage steel sculpture, and small hide rugs courtesy Katie Koch Home, New Orleans; selected area rugs courtesy NOLA Rugs, New Orleans.

ACKNOWLEDGMENTS

I AM IMMENSELY GRATEFUL to so many for their contributions to this book and to the work it describes and celebrates. None of this would be possible without the clients who task us with creating environments for living, working, playing, worshipping, and viewing art; we are honored by their faith in us. Successful buildings and interiors take teamwork, and the artisans, builders, and consultants with whom we've collaborated have been talented as well as generous players. Writer Linda O'Keeffe graciously guided this project at its inception with steady insight and good humor. At Rizzoli, publisher Charles Miers believed in my voice and editor Ron Broadhurst championed my work from the outset; without their commitment, instruction, and support, this book would not have happened. Also at Rizzoli, Maria Pia Gramaglia and Alyn Evans offered invaluable technical guidance. I admire the work of all of the photographers who have so skillfully rendered the projects, and am especially grateful to my principal photographer Pieter Estersohn, whose artistry is equaled by his broad intellect and generous spirit. Pablo Cubarle worked magic in retouching and color balancing the images, and, in my office, Sara Harper and Will Soniat provided prodigious assistance. I have treasured the many working sessions with my tireless book designer David Byars, who married the images with a nuanced language of font and white space; his methodology has remained fluid throughout. I offer my heartfelt gratitude to John Stubbs for his eloquent introduction, to my co-writer, Mayer Rus, whose gifted eye and agile mind are always accompanied with kindness and a singular wit, and to my childhood friend, Margaret Sartor, who lent her expertise with words and photographs and supported me throughout this journey. I thank my husband, Douglas Meffert, for giving me the space to dream, to obsess, to be a bit mad, and for loving me because and in spite of it all.

Most of all, I am grateful to and for my studio colleagues, both former and current, who have contributed so much of themselves to the projects we undertake, many of which are depicted herein. This book is as much yours as it is mine.

Richard Fullerton	Justin Agnew	Georgia Downs	Zeke Jordan III	Jarod Moninger
Tarra Cotterman	Kim Payne Allen	Matthew Duguid	Peter Kilgust	Robert Riccardi
Chris Loudon	Kevin Atkinson	Varuni Edussuriya	Alissa Kingsley	Chris Roche
Amy Petersen	Vince Bandy	Scott Evans	Caroline Kwong	Will Rosenthal
William Soniat, Jr.	Susan Boyd	Kevin Frank	Curtis Laub	Miriam Salles
Heather Sutton	Nichole Chauvin	Tyson Geary	Lyle LeBlanc	Michael Sewell
Sara Allen Harper	Elizabeth Chen	Andrew Graham	Lee Lormand	Kim Summerlin
Margarette Weaver	David Dieckhoff	Terrill Hewett	Karri Maggio	Jennifer Webber
Paul Zansler	Michael Diodati	Jade Jiambutr	Marty McElveen	Tom Zook

LEE LEDBETTER

First published in the United States of America in 2019 by
Rizzoli International Publications, Inc.
300 Park Avenue South
New York, NY 10010
www.rizzoliusa.com

ISBN: 978-0-8478-6211-5
LCCN: 2018953233

© 2019 Lee Ledbetter

BOOK DESIGN BY DAVID BYARS

All rights reserved. No part of this publication may be reproduced, stored in a retrieval system, or transmitted in any form or by any means, electronic, mechanical, photocopying, recording, or otherwise, without prior consent of the publisher.

Printed and bound in China

2019 2020 2021 2022 2023 / 10 9 8 7 6 5 4 3 2 1

PAGE 238 Vintage stacking tables and a Thonet chair sit in front of historical engravings in Ledbetter's former French Quarter office. **ABOVE** A table by Le Corbusier and a French giltwood mirror in the dining area of the Bayou Bonfouca residence. **ENDPAPERS** Custom *verre églomisé* panels at the Chestnut Street residence.